Issues in Education and Technology

Policy Guidelines and Strategies

edited by
Cream Wright

COMMONWEALTH SECRETARIAT

Commonwealth Secretariat
Marlborough House
Pall Mall
London SW1Y 5HX
United Kingdom

Edited, designed and originated by
BDP – Book Design and Production
Bosulval, Newmill, Penzance TR20 8XA

Printed and bound by

Whenever possible, the Commonwealth Secretariat uses paper
sourced from sustainable forests or from sources that minimise
a destructive impact on the environment.

Copies of this publication can be ordered direct from
The Publications Unit
Commonwealth Secretariat
Marlborough House
Pall Mall
London SW1Y 5HX
United Kingdom
Tel +44 (0)20 7747 6342
Fax +44 (0)20 7839 9081
e-mail r.jones-parry @commonwealth.int
Price £12.99
ISBN 0 85092 622 X

Web sites:
http://www.thecommonwealth.org/gender
http://www.thecommonwealth.org
http://www.youngcommonwealth.org

Contents

List of Figures and Tables

Tables

Foreword

Dame Veronica Sutherland
Deputy Secretary-General of the Commonwealth
Commonwealth Secretariat, London, UK

Issues in Education and Technology addresses two important topics that currently preoccupy many decision-makers. There is hardly a more topical issue in today's world than the impact of technology on society, as it fuels unprecedented changes which influence how we live and work within different countries as well as across national boundaries. These changes offer the hope of increased benefits for many countries, but they also raise fears that some developing countries will be left behind and so become even further marginalised. There is therefore a sense of urgency about the need to cope with unfolding circumstances and to seize emerging opportunities. One of the key challenges facing decision-makers everywhere is how best to harness the great potential of these rapidly unfolding technologies to the complex goals of human development.

A second topical issue for most decision-makers concerns the role of education in the development process, as we enter a new millennium. Leaders in developed and developing countries routinely express a new sense of vision about the ways in which education can empower individuals, communities and nations to make choices for their own development. This is critical in the face of global changes that place a premium on knowledge and information as the key to development. Investment in education has therefore emerged as a major priority for the political leadership in most countries. This raises difficult questions about the kind of reforms and innovations needed in education, as a precondition for any major investment of scarce resources. Underlying these questions are issues of how to spread the benefits of education to all citizens; how to improve its relevance and efficiency, and how to ensure value for money in the provision of education and the management of education systems.

In addressing these issues, *Issues in Education and Technology* uses educational analysis as a basis for exploring the role of technology in dealing with key educational problems. This approach involves a strong focus on educational issues and problems, with technology treated as a prolific tool that serves human purpose in helping to solve problems in education. This book avoids the danger of technological determinism, concentrating instead on a level-headed analysis of educational issues and technological possibilities.

I sincerely hope that this Commonwealth publication will inspire and inform decision-makers and all those concerned with investments in technology for the development of education. The jargon-free approach and careful analysis of education and technology issues from first principles is refreshing and illuminating for non-specialists. It is also my hope that the illustrative case studies from different parts of the Commonwealth will provide valuable insight into how a number of countries are dealing with the challenges involved in the strategic use of technology to improve education.

Introduction

The Background to this Book

Issues in Education and Technology is a response to the needs expressed by Commonwealth Ministers of Education at their thirteenth Triennial Conference (13CCEM) held in Botswana in July 1997. Ministers and delegation leaders were anxious that their education systems and their societies should not be left behind in the rapid advance of information and communication technology (ICT), which has profound implications for all societies in an era of globalisation. They were aware, however, that there are difficult choices to be made and complex issues to be clarified, as governments strive to take sensible decisions about investments in technology for education. There was some concern that previous investments in technology such as educational television and radio, or language laboratories, had not yielded the expected benefits for education. It was not clear whether countries should simply write off such past investments or continue to invest in trying to make them more useful. Some countries felt they would have to discard such technologies as outmoded and expensive in the face of high maintenance costs and current developments of cheaper and more sophisticated technologies in the field of ICT. There was also concern that the poor state of telecommunications infrastructure in many countries would necessitate massive investments in order to introduce the new technologies, which would largely benefit the already advantaged urban populations at the expense of deprived rDame Veronicaural communities. This involves very sensitive issues of equity, which cannot be ignored in reaching decisions about investments in technology for education.

Some countries were concerned about the possible impact of these new technologies on the social and moral development of their citizens, in view of the risks of cultural invasion posed by such technologies. They felt it was inevitable that the norms, values and lifestyles prevailing in the countries of origin of these technologies would come to dominate their societies and erode their cultural integrity. This was not a welcome prospect, and for many countries it represented a new form of cultural imperialism.

Other countries had very practical concerns about the feasibility of investing in these new technologies, because they quite simply could not afford the capital, recurrent and/or opportunity costs involved. They realised that in addition to the costs of developing the necessary infrastructure, and acquiring and maintaining the new technologies, there would be the related costs of staff training and systemic changes that invariably characterise the introduction of new technologies. They faced difficult choices and competing priorities in the fields of education and development. In many countries education systems are struggling to maintain quality; enrolment levels are still unsatisfactory; facilities and basic supplies are in a perilous state, and education budgets barely cover staff salaries. In such circumstances it is difficult to see how decision-makers could ignore these fundamental requirements and yet try to justify major investments in new technologies that could be regarded as beneficial to those already having an advantage. Indeed the message from the Education Ministers at 13CCEM, to Commonwealth Heads of Government, highlights the reminder that we still have a great deal of ground to make up in the area of basic literacy in most Commonwealth countries.

Despite these and other concerns expressed by Ministers and delegation leaders, there was also a strong awareness of the critical importance of investments in technology for education. It was felt that countries that do not make such investments risk being further marginalised in the new era of globalisation. Indeed several countries were able to cite the benefits they were beginning to derive from investments they had started to make in this area, and many had plans for such investments in the future. In several cases the role of the Commonwealth of Learning in helping countries with their distance learning projects was greatly appreciated. There was also an appreciation of the fact that with recent developments, some of the new technologies may hold the promise of feasible and more cost effective solutions to the problems of education for deprived groups and communities, as well as for education and development in general. All of this was clearly epitomised in a healthy degree of enthusiasm among Ministers and delegation leaders. There was a fairly positive instinct about the need to invest in technology for education. However, it was also clear that this enthusiasm coexisted rather uneasily with a large dose of concern and some element of scepticism. It was in view of this festering ambivalence that the Commonwealth Secretariat's Education Department decided to work on a book that would enrich the knowledge base from which key decisions can be taken about investments in technology for education.

Why this Book is Required at this Time

Changes in education are inevitable in the face of the inexorable advance of the knowledge and information age that is being fuelled by rapid developments in ICT. Decision-makers and education planners are therefore under pressure to make major changes that in most cases would amount to a quantum leap in investments in technology for education. There is a growing body of enthusiasts, and a rapidly expanding literature, extolling the virtues of such investments and warning of the consequences of failure to invest now. This multiplicity of advocates has in fact compounded the problem for decision-makers, who are now less certain about answers to investment questions regarding what kinds of technologies, in what quantities, at what levels and for what purposes. Part of the problem is that much of the literature tends to be couched in the language of vogue technology, with which most decision-makers and planners are uncomfortable. Some of this literature is little more than commercial hype, which ignores fundamental education issues that need careful consideration. There is therefore an increasing need for publications that provide a clear and dispassionate insight into key issues and problems which relate to making these inevitable changes in education through major investments in technology. This is one reason why the present book is timely.

At the other extreme, there is a small but assertive sceptic literature that cautions against an unquestioning embrace of the new technologies. Decision-makers cannot afford to ignore the sceptics completely, because their messages raise key issues to do with equity, cultural integrity, and the negative aspects of technology in economic and social development. The ideology underpinning this kind of scepticism may appear to be idealistic or even naïve, but the issues involved need to be taken seriously in the difficult business of making decisions about investing in technology for education. It is therefore important that decision-makers and planners should have access to publications that highlight these critical issues without wrapping them in sceptical ideology.

Perhaps the most important reason for the publication of *Issues in Education and Technology* is the need to raise awareness of the fact that the changes involved in investing in technology for education, at the dawn of the twenty-first century, are of an unprecedented complexity and magnitude. This is not simply because of the difficult choices involved, or the sophistication of the latest technologies, or the high level of investments that may be required. It is due rather to the profound implications of such changes for the whole education process and their potential impact on the development of communities and nations everywhere in the new era of globalisation. It is therefore critical for decision-makers and planners to appreciate that in this case change is not simply a matter of an incremental use of various technologies in education. It is not even a matter of wholesale investment in certain new technologies such as computers. Rather it is about the role of technology in promoting deep systemic changes in education to meet the challenges of a new era. It is about using technology to enhance the way we deal with key issues of access and equity, management and efficiency, pedagogy and quality, as well as preparing citizens for an era of globalisation that will be dominated by technologies related to knowledge and information. In other words, we are confronted with the need for fundamental changes in education and development, rather than a need for changes in technology *per se*. *Issues in Education and Technology* therefore gives top priority to education and development issues, as a basis for exploring the ways in which technology in general can play a role in promoting and sustaining constructive and manageable change in education for development. It puts technology in context, as a tool that serves human purposes, rather than as an end in itself. It explores the place of a wide range of technologies in serving education, and does not confine itself to ICT. Through this kind of analysis, it helps to promote an understanding of the ways in which different technologies can interface with education and development in different societies to achieve various objectives.

In an era of technological surfeit it is easy to perceive developments in this field as a linear progression in which each new technology represents an improvement on the previous ones. The inevitable implication is that the latest is the best and those who do not keep up with the trends will lose out in the development process. Although some of this is true to some extent, issues of technology and development are in fact far more complex. Technological evolution is not a simple story of linear progression. It is more akin to a series of cyclic loops that are constantly in motion and moving mainly in a forward direction – sometimes rolling and more recently leaping forward. Most new technologies have definite advantages over the old ones that they seek to replace. However, new technologies may also bring new problems and result in the loss of some advantages associated with the older technologies.

Technology is always a means to an end, never an end in itself, so its impact on human society is far more important than its intrinsic characteristics. We must be wary of falling into the trap of technological determinism. There is nothing *inherently* valuable about technology. It acquires value to the extent that it proves useful for and beneficial to human purposes. Therefore it is important that in dealing with education and technology, our primary concern and starting point should be that of human purpose. What are the goals and objectives of education, and what are the ways in which various technologies can help us to achieve them? At the same time, however, we need to keep in mind that in every country the goals and objectives set for education are profoundly influenced by trends in society at large. In turn, these trends are now being influenced as never before by changes in technology. From this perspective what is critical for education is not necessarily the latest or the most sophisticated technology, but the most appropriate technology for the purpose at hand. Responsible decision-making also requires that the need for investment in technology should be balanced against other educational needs in order to determine what is affordable. New technologies invariably bring new demands that need to be kept in view and balanced against their possible benefits. This book explores these and many other related issues, in order to strengthen the knowledge base from which decisions are made about investments in technology for education and development.

The Purpose and Scope of this Book

The purpose of *Issues in Education and Technology* is to provide insight into and understanding of the key issues in education and development that are increasingly making it imperative for nations to review their policies and strategies concerning investment in technology for education and development. In this context it offers policy guidelines and practical strategies for those who have to make major decisions about investments in, and use of, technology for education systems and institutions.

In the interest of clarity, it is important to highlight what the book does not set out to achieve as well as what it does seek to achieve. This book does not set out to *prescribe* solutions, but rather to offer a basis for making choices between viable options. In presenting these options for consideration, it tries to highlight the consequences and implications of different choices. *Issues in Education and Technology* is not concerned with presenting a catalogue of new technologies and what they can do for education. It is not intended to be an 'expert guide' to the available technologies and their use in education, nor is it meant to be a guide to 'value for money' in selecting hardware, software, or staff training programmes. Rather, its concern is with exploring technology issues relating to education and development, in order to highlight the need for sound policies and pragmatic strategies relating to investment in technology for education.

This book is neither theoretical nor academic. It seeks to promote informed decision-making in a very pragmatic manner by dealing with concrete problems relating to education and the role of technology. It highlights key issues related to policy and strategy, and outlines various considerations and arguments that are most relevant to the challenges that face decision-makers in this area. These issues and arguments are grounded in the social and economic evolution of technologies related to education and development. They are also very pertinent to the problems and challenges in the field of education and development at the dawn of the twenty-first century.

Issues in Education and Technology also seeks to be of practical relevance by outlining examples of current practices, through carefully selected case studies. However, these case studies are not meant to serve as examples of best practice that should necessarily be copied. Rather they provide wholesome examples of policy, strategy and practice in the use of technology for certain educational objectives in particular contexts. For instance, the case study from Singapore (page 91) deals with the use of technology for management of the education system. It provides us with a holistic picture of policy decisions, implementation strategies and practical outcomes, against a background of wider development trends in Singapore society.

The overall aim of *Issues in Education and Technology* is to contribute to a greater awareness and confidence-building for those who are not technology specialists, but who have the responsibility for making critical decisions on investments in technology for education and development. It puts human purpose firmly at the centre of such decision-making, and takes the major challenges facing education as the starting point for exploring the place of technology in education systems.

Orientation, Structure and Content

Issues in Education and Technology starts from first principles, exploring the key issues that link education, technology and development. This provides a macro-landscape that serves as a framework for understanding the place of different technologies in education systems and processes linked to development. Within this framework we outline the ways in which evolving technologies have been of use and value in the process of education, as well as in driving the development process generally. It then becomes possible to link human purpose and educational goals much more systematically with various kinds of technologies, and to have a clearer sense of what kinds of policies and strategies may be most relevant for different societies at different points in their development.

The book is structured in three broad sections that cover the main areas in which technology can have the greatest influence and most decisive impact on education. These critical areas are access and equity; management and efficiency, and pedagogy and quality. In each area the main issues relating to education and development are first outlined and explored in order to provide a shared understanding. There follows an analysis of the technologies involved in order to highlight their current and potential usefulness in education and development. The analysis is not only set in functional and organisational terms, but also takes account of historical, cultural and socio-economic contexts. After this analysis there is an outline of the main challenges that decision-makers must address in dealing with policies and strategies for investment in technology that would promote positive change in education for development. Finally, attention is given to the key issue of formulating policies and strategies in this area. Each section of the book ends with one or more illustrative case studies, specially commissioned from a Commonwealth country.

Issues in Education and Technology draws extensively on experiences of Commonwealth countries which, given their diversity and varied stages of development in the use of technologies for educational purposes, provide a particularly rich resource base. Case studies in the form of country papers were prepared by Ministries of Education and submitted to the Commonwealth Secretariat for 13CCEM. In addition, in 1998 the Secretariat commissioned several more focused studies to explore the state of development in certain critical areas. These papers form the case studies in this book.

Who is this Book Aimed at?

Issues in Education and Technology is intended for use by a wide range of policy makers, planners and practitioners in education and development. It should be of value to Ministers of Education and their senior advisers, whose primary concern is setting broad policies and making investment choices for education and development. It should also be of value to educational planners and senior administrators responsible for designing and managing education systems. Heads of institutions and classroom practitioners should also find it useful, especially in decentralised education systems where they may have to make key decisions relating to the use of technology.

Beyond national education systems, *Issues in Education and Technology* should assist other ministries concerned with national development policies, since the issues involved have profound implications for development generally. Besides, investment decisions of this kind are not purely a matter for education ministries. National policies on science and technology, as well as development strategies, will have a bearing on investment decisions relating to the use of technology in education. It is hoped that this book will inform and influence key officials outside education, in a manner that will be of benefit to educational goals and objectives.

Issues in Education and Technology should also be useful to external development partner agencies seeking to assist countries in the area of investment in technology for education. At the very least it should help to promote greater sensitivity to the challenges which many developing countries face in making choices about this kind of investment. What some external partner agencies enthuse about as the self-evident benefits of technology in education may present developing countries with serious dilemmas relating to equity and opportunity costs. Similarly, despite the possibilities of moving towards adopting the latest technologies, the pace of change needs to be strategically managed in most developing countries' education systems. Most developing countries are also extremely sensitive about innovations that deepen their long-term dependency on external assistance.

Commercial purveyors of technology may also find this book useful. It might at least help to make them more conscious of, and sympathetic to, the difficulties that face decision-makers in dealing with policies and strategies relating to investments in technology for education. Manufacturers and service providers can play a major role in enlightening decision-makers about technological possibilities for tackling various educational problems. They can also help to deal with the peculiar requirements of some countries through design and development of customised equipment, software or systems. However, it is important that these manufacturers and service providers develop an empathetic understanding of the many difficulties and challenges facing decision-makers in education.

How to Use this Book

Decision-makers and planners concerned with investments in technology for education, as well as practitioners who work in the field of education and technology, can use this book in two major ways. First, they can use it to gain greater insight into the rationale for investing in technology for education. Discussions with policy-makers in various countries suggest that while investments are being made in some form of technology for education, the underlying rationale, policy objectives and strategic plan are not always very clear. There is often a sense that pressure for change and the need to appear progressive have led to hasty decisions based more on the attractiveness of technology than on sound insight into educational needs and development goals. That is why *Issues in Education and Technology* seeks to provide appropriate insight by arguing from first principles rather than from a position of simple technological advocacy. It is important to help countries differentiate between the various education objectives and development goals for which investments might need to be made in technology for education. This book therefore takes education and development needs as its starting point, rather than being based primarily on what technology can do for us.

The second way of using *Issues in Education and Technology* is as a source of holistic examples of the manner in which technology is currently being used for specific purposes in particular Commonwealth countries. This is facilitated by the case studies which have been carefully selected to reflect the issues of access and equity; management and efficiency, quality and pedagogy. Each case study provides a detailed analysis of the issues involved; the underlying principles, and the difficulties experienced, as well as the policy decisions and practical strategies involved. The case studies therefore reflect holistic examples with positive and negative aspects highlighted for consideration.

1 Education, Technology and Development Revisited

A Review of the Links

There is an important three-way link between education, technology and development that is becoming critical in an age of globalisation. Technology has always been a major driving force in the development of nations. At the same time the direction and pace of technological progress have been greatly influenced by the development goals and policies that constitute every nation's vision for the future. The link between technology and development is widely understood and has long been a feature of policy-making and strategic planning in most countries. There are very few countries in which development goals and policies do not embrace some strategy or direction for technological progress, or for the application of technology to achieve set objectives. In the same way, policies and strategies in the areas of science and technology are usually anchored in a vision of development for the society. This is clearly illustrated in the country papers for 13CCEM, extracts of which are reproduced here.

The necessary link between technology and development is widely perceived as education, which has long been acknowledged as an important source of the kind of knowledge-making that underpins progress in science and technology. For some nations it was important to be at the cutting edge of technological development in order to retain competitive advantage in the fields of socio-economic and cultural development, or to assert a military superiority that would safeguard their society. For others the main challenge was to ensure that they were in a strong position to make systematic use of existing technology to increase economic productivity and improve the quality of life for their population. For another group of nations the top priority was how best to take advantage of the new opportunities offered by technology, to assist their rapid transformation into modern, newly industrialised societies. Yet other nations were concerned with the challenge of using technology to combat deep and persistent under-development in their societies, or to catch up in a perceived development

'The basic objectives of the Technology Policy are the development of indigenous technology and efficient absorption and adaptation of imported technology to national priorities and resources.'
(India Country Paper)

'The broad objective of the Government is to increase the role of science and technology in the attainment of economic and social development, by bringing about social transformation … and improving the quality of life.'
(Jamaica Country Paper)

'Any type of development without the help of science and technology is not possible. It is therefore essential to provide high national priority to scientific and technological considerations in the overall development strategy of the country.'
(Bangladesh Country Paper)

race. Despite such a diverse range of priorities and areas of concern, nations typically turned to their education systems to help prepare the specialist manpower and produce the kind of knowledge that would harness technology to their development goals and priorities. Their national policies and strategies clearly sought to link educational goals and objectives to those of technology and development.

Later on, it became increasingly evident that while the build-up of specialist manpower may be necessary for some aspects of development, it does not in itself provide an adequate platform for achieving meaningful and balanced development. The need to prepare non-specialists for a society dominated by technology, and the need to keep technology within manageable social and political boundaries, helped to broaden nations' concern with linking education to technology and development. Thus, in addition to educating technology specialists, it became important to educate policymakers and the general population about technology, and to do so in a manner that would prepare them to cope with various social and political roles in a technology-dominated future. Technology increasingly came to be regarded as an integral part of general education. Major initiatives were taken to diversify general education systems and incorporate relevant aspects of technology in the education provided for all learners in the system.

'national aspiration for development reflects the need to increase substantially the national stocks of technicians, engineers, technologists and scientists' (Pakistan Country Paper)

The emphasis was on using education to serve the goals and objectives of technology and development. Education was expected to prepare a cadre of specialists in technology, as well as to produce a technologically enlightened citizenry. There was only a weak link and some token concern with using technology to serve educational goals and objectives. This was mainly confined to a rather moribund field known as 'educational technology'.

It is important to appreciate that the current arguments for investing in technology for education are very different from those used in the past to make a case for the field of educational technology. The old rationale was largely about improved pedagogy and so focused mainly on teaching and learning aids. In contrast, the new rationale for investing in technology for education is much wider and deals with more fundamental and complex issues. This makes it imperative for all governments to act more systematically in addressing the issue of policies and strategies for investment in technology related to education and development. We live in a new age and we need to take a new approach to dealing with these issues as we tackle the major challenges facing us in education and development.

We are experiencing a steady progression from a purely technological age to what has been termed the 'information and knowledge' age. The key technological developments of the recent past are not predominantly about economic productivity, but more to do with innovative ways of producing, storing, transmitting, accessing and using knowledge and information. It is generally acknowledged that these developments are the direct result of the very rapid and revolutionary advances in information communication technologies (ICT) of the past two decades. A recent phenomenon is the steady decline in value of most manufactured goods and physical assets as automation has peaked and economic valuation has altered quite radically in favour of knowledge-based services.

Nations now gain a competitive edge through their capacity to innovate and stay ahead of developments that pertain to information and communication technologies. In many ways information and knowledge have become the new gold standards that determine prosperity and security. Thus the most important assets of nations are not raw materials, physical goods or economic production, but human resources keyed into the information and knowledge revolution. Increasingly, the competitiveness and prosperity of nations are critically dependent on the level of education and training of their population, and particularly their capacity to cope with, and take advantage of, the continuous explosion in knowledge and information that is readily accessible through the new technologies. A key implication of these changes is that the role of education and training in development has become more critical than ever before. There is a new and fundamental sense in which *education is development*!

As societies progress from a purely technological age to the new age of globalisation, the most important need is for technology to serve education and development goals. Knowledge and information are the new forms of wealth and hold the key as the driving force for the development of individuals, communities and nations. The main challenge therefore is how to ensure that the population in general can have access to the means of developing the necessary skills to cope with and function effectively in the new age of information and knowledge. These 'how to' questions are typically about technology. The challenge is to use technology to facilitate the education and training of the population for the new age of globalisation.

Essentially this provides the strongest linkage for education in the three-way link that binds education, technology and development. This is a vital argument and represents the strongest rationale for investing in technology for education. It is a deep and systemic argument that ties investment in technology not only with progress in education, but (more importantly) with the development process itself. It represents the key strand in a reciprocal link through which education, technology and development can become mutually reinforcing within a dynamic framework for progress. It also represents what is increasingly seen as a fundamental human right for every citizen to have access to the means of connecting with the forces that shape their life-chances in a global era. This in a sense equates education with empowerment for development.

Why Invest in Technology for Education?

Some nations may decide to invest in technology for education for the 'glitz factor': The technology is there; it is fashionable to have the latest and the best, and it gives a sense of progress to use state-of-the-art technology. This can be described as the 'technology for its own sake' rationale. Other nations may base their investment decisions on the genuine case for improving the efficiency of their education systems or for some other benefits intrinsic to education. For instance, data bases and computerised records in education systems have clear advantages and benefits. This is the 'technology for educational benefits' rationale. A third rationale may be external to education and concerned with developing skills for the labour market. Each of these three rationales can be a valid basis for making decisions about investment in technology for education, but none is sufficient to provide an imperative for nations to make such investments in a systematic and sustained manner.

In contrast, the three-way link gives a necessary and sufficient rationale that makes it imperative for nations to invest in technology for education if they are serious about national development in the new era of globalisation. As the process of globalisation advances and reaches the farthest corners of human settlement, individuals and communities will become more assertive about their right to have access to the means of survival in the new dispensation. It will no longer be a matter of whether they should have access to the kind of education that empowers them for development, but how best to ensure that they do have such access. The use of public and private resources to facilitate such access will invariably raise issues of equity and social cohesion as well as efficiency and cost effectiveness. Technology will play a major role in the way countries deal with these and other emerging challenges. It will therefore require sound policies and pragmatic strategies to ensure the best investment decisions.

Such decisions have far-reaching consequences for individual and community development, as well as for social cohesion, economic competitiveness and the social progress of nations. Against this background, it is clear that decisions about investing in technology for education are not simply a matter for education policy-makers and officials.

The Basics of Technology and Development

Technology may be defined in simple terms as 'a means of doing or making things and acting on our world'. In this sense it is an important feature that distinguishes humans from most other animals. It is also a major characteristic that reflects the level of development of one society or nation in relation to another. Hence when we rank countries in terms of development, our judgment is based partly on their level of technological progress. Most countries therefore place great emphasis on technology as a critical factor in their development strategies. Technology helps to determine the level and efficiency of production of goods and services in society. It is therefore one of the most important factors that shape a country's competitiveness in the global market-place. Technology also has a great influence on the general quality of life in any society through its impact on work and leisure patterns, living conditions and environmental safety. It is therefore a defining feature of contemporary culture. Table 1.1 illustrates the impact of technology on development.

Table 1.1 The Impact of Technology on Development

Development area	Kind of impact
Economic Development	Improved efficiency in production of goods and services, leading to advantages in areas of trade, investment and wealth creation.
Social Development	Changing patterns of work, relationships and income levels, leading to changes in the distribution of wealth, status and power.
Cultural Development	Changing settlement patterns, resulting in changes to environment, leisure activities and general quality of life.

Technological progress in any country usually depends on policies and strategies put in place by political leaders as well as by professional decision-makers and practitioners in various fields relating to the production of goods and services. In this regard there are, in theory, at least three broad principles that can be used to guide technological development. First, there is the principle of endogenous development, or 'home-grown' technology, which uses indigenous knowledge, skills and resources to advance the production of goods and services. It is important to appreciate that, in a historical sense, every society has its own indigenous technology that relates very closely to the local culture and environment. These may not be the most advanced or efficient technologies, but they usually give a strong indication of how to improve technology in an appropriate way for that society. It is also important to appreciate that while technological progress in some societies has been largely driven by endogenous efforts, every society has had to borrow from others in the process of technological development. However, this has not produced an open system of exchange where each country can freely borrow and adapt technology from others. Ownership and control of technologies represent a major factor in the relative power and competitiveness of nations in the modern world, and one of the most significant features that divide developing countries from developed ones.

The second principle is wholesale acquisition of technology from outside the country. This involves importing and making direct use of products, processes, techniques and services that have been developed by another country. It is usually the key principle underlying rapid modernisation, in which advanced goods and services are simply purchased and transplanted into a society that has the requisite wealth to afford this approach. For development purposes this principle carries an expectation that technology will take root through the imported products, processes and services. It is one of the main principles that underlie and drive international trade or the exchange of goods and services.

The third principle is that of selective borrowing and adaptation. This involves importing certain strategically selected products, processes, techniques and services, which are then modified or combined in some way for use in the local socio-economic and cultural context. This is a case of grafting useful technologies from outside to what already exists in the society.

It is essential that countries are clear about which major principle or combination of principles they are adopting as part of the strategy for investing in technology that will make a change in education and development. This obviously depends on such factors as the strength and reliability of their indigenous technology; their purchasing power to import external technologies on a substantial scale, and the mix of resources and expertise that can enable them to adapt external technologies to local needs. As stated above, ownership of technologies and the terms governing their exchange constitute a critical divide between developed and developing countries. High emphasis on importing external technologies has implications for increased pace of development as well as for increased dependency on others if these technologies do not take root in the local economy. Conversely, high emphasis on endogenous technological development has implications for slow growth as well as for greater self-reliance. The adaptation of external technologies pre-supposes a certain level of technological capabilities in the local labour pool, which may not exist. Factors such as these are important in making decisions about national strategies for technology and development. Table 1.2 (page 22) summarises the three broad principles used to guide technological development.

Historically, much attention has been given to those aspects of technology that relate to economic productivity. Therefore the landmarks of technological progress tend to be defined in terms of phenomena such as agrarian reform, industrial revolution, mass production and automation. However, human progress, and the technologies that underpin it, need not be measured purely in terms of economic productivity. Indeed the major landmarks of technological development have also highlighted critical social and cultural changes in society. They have reshaped work-force organisation; changed the labour market, and influenced working relations as well as the work environment. More importantly, major advances in technology have greatly influenced land-use and human settlement patterns. They have also had a major impact on the distribution of wealth and power in society, as well as on family and social life generally. In these and many other respects, it is evident that the impact of technology is holistic and all-pervading. Technology affects all aspects of our lives in very profound ways, as individuals, families, communities, nation-states and even as 'families of nations' such as the Commonwealth. In its broadest sense therefore, technology is development!

Table 1.2 The Guiding Principles for Technological Development

Kind of principle	Outline of the principle
Endogenous development	This is about using and improving on home-grown technology, which is an integral part of the local culture; e.g. India has several centuries of civilisation during which its own traditional technologies have played a major role.
Development through wholesale acquisition of technology from external sources	Countries that can afford this often depend on the lasting impact from such importation of external technologies; e.g. Brunei is in a position to import external technologies on a massive scale in order to transform the pace of development.
Development through selective borrowing and adaptation of external technologies	Where a high level of skills is available locally, a country can embark on selective borrowing and adaptation of technologies most relevant to its requirements.

Taking a New Look at Technology and Education

When we explore the use of technology in education from first principles, it seems quite evident that we are concerned mainly with ways of communicating information and knowledge. This raises the issue of language as a means of communication, which is central to the progress of human society. It is through language and communication that we acquire the kind of knowledge and understanding which help us to function as productive members of our communities. These are the tools that enable us to access the centuries of accumulated knowledge that is the heritage of human progress. They hold the key to our ability to generate new knowledge that can be passed on to others and made available to future generations, and they serve as a major comparative indicator of national development. Countries with low levels of literacy, for instance, tend to be relatively under-developed compared with those with high levels of literacy. Even within countries one of the greatest measures of inequality is when segments of the population remain illiterate in the face of sophisticated progress for other population groups.

Therefore, when we explore the use of technology in education, attention should be given to the history of technologies relating to information and communication, and the ways in which they have influenced the development process. It is this dimension of technology, and its implications for education, that is the main focus of this book.

We live in an era of rapid technological change that promises ever-increasing levels of prosperity and growth for some countries, while threatening a greater degree of marginalisation for others. This paradox has become a defining characteristic of nations in a new age of technological 'haves' and 'have-nots' that is most evident in the area of information and communication. Hence some analysts talk of 'information rich' and 'information poor' countries as the new divide in the world. To understand the full implications of this situation for education and national development, we need to explore briefly the rise of the new technologies that are related to information and communication in the broadest sense.

For educational purposes, technology is not only about hardware and software, but also, and importantly, about procedures, processes, structures, systems and patterns of use. In educational terms, technology is about means towards certain ends, having largely to do with thought processes, information flows and human communication. To the extent that technology can bring about improvements and advantages in these areas, it can enhance the process of education. It is therefore important to analyse changes in technology in terms of their impact on information flows and human communication, as well as human thought processes.

Language is at the heart of human communication, and is therefore the main vehicle for every form of education. The natural state of language use (the spoken word) has a range of advantages and disadvantages when used on its own, as in face-to-face encounters. For instance, it can be highly interactive and takes place in real time, but it is also time-bound and confined to a specific location. A basic contention of this book is that the history of technological development in the field of information and communication is fundamentally about efforts to overcome these barriers of time and space. It can also be argued that every major technological development has not only brought advantages, but also introduced new problems to contend with.

The invention of writing (and reading) marked the first major advancement in the use of language for information and communication. The capacity to encode thought and ideas in writing made it possible to produce, store, transmit and retrieve knowledge and information in a much more permanent and reliable form than through 'word of mouth' and human memory. Thus in the educational process, once learners master the business of reading and writing they achieve a significant breakthrough from the world of oral tradition. A new world opens up for them in terms of their ability to communicate with the past, present and future. This not only enables them to access information and knowledge, but also to create information and knowledge.

Writing is one of the most important milestones in the use of technology in education, and its impact is relevant today. In development terms, there is a major difference between pre-literate and literate societies. Even within a given nation, those communities that have yet to benefit from writing and reading are always at a great disadvantage in relation to the rest of society. It is important to appreciate, however, that while the invention of writing offered distinct communication advantages over simple 'word of mouth', it also had relative disadvantages. For instance, communication by writing results in a loss of the interactive and real-time dimension that is a significant feature of face-to-face encounters. More importantly, in terms of education and development it opened up the first major divide (literate versus non-literate) that still plagues us today.

Many later developments in technology can be classified as elaborations of the reading and writing milestone. Thus the invention of the printing machine made possible the kind of mass production and dissemination of information and knowledge that was not available with manual writing. In principle this opened the way for a system of mass education and the widespread dissemination of knowledge and information. However, the production and dissemination of knowledge was still impeded by barriers of time and space. Indeed, educational book publishing is still a fairly elaborate process with substantial time lapse between completion of a manuscript and printing of the book. Then there is the need to physically transport books to various destinations in the marketing chain before they eventually become available to the end users. All of this, of course, involves significant costs. Therefore, it can be argued that while the invention of printing opened up new possibilities and made available new opportunities for mass education, it also introduced a new divide in the development process. Essentially this is a divide that is still with us, and is best defined in terms of those who can afford ready access to a wide range of educational materials (books, etc.) and those who cannot. The issue of access to books and learning materials is one of the major determinants of quality and effective learning in any education system.

It is also the case that printing and the publishing industry have precipitated new power structures, in terms of ownership of (and control over) information and knowledge. The powerful determine what counts as worthwhile knowledge that should be published for educational use, while the powerless are often reduced to being passive consumers of other people's knowledge. Many countries and local communities still face a major problem in this area, in terms of the relevance of the educational materials available to them. To the extent that they cannot afford to develop and produce their own materials, they could become trapped in a cycle of cultural and intellectual dependency that has a negative impact on education and development. The invention of a wider range of reprographic technologies, including photocopiers, ink duplicators and desktop publishing, could have an ameliorating effect on this kind of problem, but it is still an issue for decision-makers to take into account when dealing with investments in technology for education. The case study on electronic publishing illustrates some of the exciting and promising possibilities for addressing these problems through modern information and communication technologies.

Other technological developments that help to bridge the gap of time and space without putting non-literate persons at a disadvantage are the radio, telephone and television. In each case there is some progress as well as some new problems. New opportunities for mass communication were created by the invention of these technologies. Radio and television provide mainly one-way mass communication (although two-way versions exist); the telephone is the prime example of real-time interactive communication across space. The wired versions of these technologies have restrictions in terms of the spread of their physical grid. There are also major restrictions relating to capital and operating costs of these technologies, for the end users as well as the providers of the services. Invention of wireless versions of these technologies marked a critical milestone in information and communication, as the most remote rural communities became able, for instance, to access radio broadcasts through transistor radios. Also, the wide availability of cheap power cells (batteries) and such inventions as the clockwork radio, which relies on human energy (winding up) rather than power cells, have helped to bring costs down. It is fair to say, however, that for many reasons, in most countries the potentials of these technologies have never been fully exploited for education and development.

A third category of technological developments relates mainly to human thought processes. This includes audio/video recorders and computers, which make it possible to store and retrieve information in a more reliable manner than through the human memory. This category includes information and data processing technologies such as calculators and computers. Generally all technologies that have to do with artificial intelligence would also fall into this category.

Subsequent technological developments in information and communication have to do with breaking down old barriers of time and space. They make it possible to generate, store, transmit, access, retrieve and process information and knowledge at increased speeds, and with increased efficiency and flexibility. In short, current developments in technology have opened up almost unlimited possibilities for us in terms of information flow and human communication, as well as in the area of human thought processes. In turn, these possibilities hold out great promise for what we can do in education if we invest properly in technology. Hence the current enthusiasm and strong advocacy for investing in technology for education and development.

In the face of such enthusiasm and advocacy we need to be reminded that our primary focus and purpose have to do with education and development. Despite the attractive promises of technology, we know that there are no simple solutions to the complex issues and challenges in these areas. As Malcolm Skilbeck expressed it at 13CCEM in Botswana, 'What goes on in even the poorest school is infinitely more complex than what a powerful computer can do!'

2 Technology for Access and Equity in Education

Understanding the Issues

Why Education Matters

Decisions about investing in technology for education are not purely a matter for the Ministry of Education. Such decisions depend on broad national development policies and involve other ministries including Finance, Economic Planning, Telecommunications and Development. It is therefore important to highlight not only key educational issues, but also the development-related arguments that can be used to justify national investment in technology for education. Moreover, in a climate of intense competition for scarce resources, the Education sector cannot assume that its importance is self-evident, nor take it for granted that its goals and priorities are shared by other sectors. Therefore there is a need to build cross-sector support for national investment in technology for education. There is also a need to advocate at the highest levels for top priority to be given to such investments. This is why the Ministers of Education meeting at the 13CCEM in Botswana in 1997 decided to send a message and a plea on these matters to their heads of government who met shortly after in Edinburgh. The case for education and for investment in technology needs to be made repeatedly to various interest groups and stakeholders.

Despite a plethora of problems and widespread criticism, education remains one of the most powerful instruments for human development. It is the prime means through which every society initiates its young into a way of life that defines its heritage and contemporary values, as well as its aspirations for the future. Education is also the fundamental mechanism through which individuals learn many of the skills needed to function successfully in various social and economic roles. In socio-economic terms, education is a proven catalyst that moves individuals and communities out of poverty and ignorance, into an improved quality of life. It is a lifeline of hope for families and communities trapped in conditions of impoverishment and disadvantage. It has been shown to be the most important factor that determines differences in future incomes and lifetime earnings of individuals. It is also widely regarded as a key factor in the competitiveness of communities and nations.

In cultural terms, education serves as a window through which our imagination and curiosity can take flight into the unknown and enhance our creativity. It is the key that unlocks the treasure within every human being, thereby helping individuals to achieve their full development potential. It encompasses the greatest legacy inherited by each new generation, as well as the greatest investment that each succeeding generation can make in its children and to the future of society. It has become the most important single factor that helps each generation to improve on the gains and achievements of its predecessors. In essence education is an important determinant of life chances and quality of life for individuals, communities and whole nations. It has critical implications for the economic growth, social development and cultural integrity of every nation. It is therefore a highly political and often highly politicised issue in the development debate in most countries.

Access is definitely one of the factors that loom large in the current political debate on education. Providing opportunities for people to participate in and benefit from education is widely regarded as one of the most important duties of governments throughout the world. Such provision has become a government obligation that is particularly strong in the early and formative years of young people. Hence most governments are committed in principle to providing educational opportunities for their school-aged population, up to a certain basic minimum level. Many countries also have legislation which makes it compulsory for children of school age to attend school. Increasingly, this notion of commitment to providing a basic level of education has become enshrined in the social contract between governments and their peoples. Education therefore ranks among the highest priorities of social demand regularly put upon governments. The demand for education, and the obligation to provide for it, rest on the notion of schooling as preparation for life. Individuals, families, communities and governments all have vested interests in preparation for life. This represents one of the main rationales for public as well as private investment in basic schooling. In addition, most governments accord high priority to education because of its role in building human resource capacity for development.

Beyond schooling there is a much broader concept of education which translates as a lifelong process of self-development. Governments tend to be more ambivalent about provision when it comes to this broader concept of education. It is an issue that is fundamental to the distribution of wealth and development opportunities in society, and an underlying cause of much social unrest and protests about social justice. Therefore access to education is portrayed by some advocates as one of the basic human rights in the modern world. Yet despite this common acceptance of the central importance of access to education, it remains a major problem that thwarts community and national development efforts and frustrates individual ambitions.

The Fundamentals of Access

Access is about both provision and uptake of opportunities for education. It is also about much more than initial enrolment in school, which means that basic enrolment data do not tell the full story on access. What is far more important than initial enrolment is the ability to stay in school and complete a prescribed cycle of learning. In this regard, persistence is a key factor in access to education. Ideally the problem of access, for the school-aged population at least, can be dealt with by providing enough school places to accommodate all those in this category. This has proved to be an elusive ideal, even for the developed and wealthy countries. Besides, provision of schools in itself does not guarantee that all learners will make use of them. There are many sound reasons why available opportunities are not always fully utilised. It is therefore becoming clear that different kinds of provisions must be made to meet different requirements of learners. Expansion of the one-size-fits-all model of formal schooling can no longer be regarded as the ultimate solution to the problem of access in any society.

For far too long, access has been narrowly equated with formal school enrolment. There are in fact several fundamental issues relating to the concept of access that need to be clearly understood and appreciated by decision-makers. First, despite the physical origins of the term, 'access' in education is not simply about entering a building or facility that we call a school, and taking part in what goes on inside. Nor is it just about being able to make use of a teacher or facilitator of learning. The core essence of access in education is about *being in a position to acquire knowledge and information*. While we have become used to the convention that this acquisition takes place in institutions and is normally facilitated by teachers, there is nothing sacrosanct about such formal arrangements. Society therefore needs to conceive of educational access in the broadest possible terms, as *enabling individuals to acquire the knowledge and skills that they require or desire for different purposes.*

The second key issue relating to the concept of access stems from the limitations of a focus on institutions (schools, colleges, etc.) as the prime locus for education. In the face of demographic pressures, shortage of teachers and other constraints facing these institutions, it is now evident that there will always be a residual proportion of the population in many Commonwealth countries that cannot be accommodated in these institutions. Indeed in some countries with high percentages of over-aged pupils and high repetition taking up school places, it is unlikely that the whole of the school-age population can be enrolled in schools in the foreseeable future. The gross enrolment ratios (GER) (Table 2.1) and net enrolment ratios (NER) (Table 2.2, page 31) shown for Commonwealth countries, highlight the disparities between countries as well as the persistent under-enrolment in some countries. These figures also show that as we progress from the primary or first level of education there is less systematic and sustained provision for the great majority of citizens. Essentially then, those who are outside the school-age population are in a worse position when it comes to access to the kind of knowledge and information that they require or desire. In most Commonwealth countries, provision for adult and continuing education has very low priority and public resources such as libraries tend to be poorly funded. Therefore, we are confronted with the basic and fundamental issue of *alternative provisions for access to education*. This issue needs to be understood not in terms of make-do solutions or inferior versions of what takes place in formal schools, but in terms of achieving comparable goals through different (and more appropriate) arrangements and means. The goal of enabling individuals to acquire worthwhile knowledge and information should be at the heart of alternative provisions. An important challenge in terms of access is how to ensure that those who are outside the formal system can be provided with alternative means and opportunities for acquiring the knowledge and information they need to realise their full potential for development.

A third, and increasingly important, issue is the need to provide those already within the education system with access to knowledge and information that cannot be found in their institutions. The continuing explosion in knowledge and information means that teachers are no longer the sole purveyors of what learners need to know. Besides, qualified and trained teachers are far from equitably distributed between institutions or between countries. Learners in many institutions and in many countries do not have access to what they need, because they do not have capable teachers. In much the same way, institutions have different levels of teaching and learning resources, so learners do not have equitable access to what they require. However, even the most resourceful educational institutions can no longer claim to have within their walls all the knowledge and information that their learners need. In fact this has always been recognised by the more progressive schools, in which field trips, outside visits and the use of external resource persons have been a regular feature of the curriculum. As Roy Williams points out in his case study of South Africa (page 43), *'the borders of the school should not be the borders of learning'*. A critical challenge for access in the formal education system, therefore, is to reach out beyond the boundaries of these institutions in order to tap various other sources of knowledge and information, for the benefit of learners.

Table 2.1 Gross Enrolment Ratios for Commonwealth Countries, by Level

Countries	Pre-primary	First level	Second level	Third level
Antigua and Barbuda	–[1]	–	–	–
Australia (1996)[2]	78	103	153	75.6
The Bahamas (1995)	10	100	86	–
Bangladesh (1990)	–	69	21	4.4
Barbados (1995)	–	–	–	29.4
Belize (1994)	27	121	49	–
Botswana (1996)	–	112	66	5.8
Britain (1995)	29	116	133	49.5
Brunei Darussalam (1996)	54	107	77	6.6
Cameroon (1994)	11	88	27	–
Canada (1995)	64	106	–	90.2
Cyprus (1995)	60	100	97	20.0
Dominica	–	–	–	–
Fiji (1992)	15	128	64	–
The Gambia (1995)	–	77	25	–
Ghana (1991)	–	76	37	–
Grenada	–	–	–	–
Guyana (1995)	84	95	87	9.7
India (1996)	5	101	49	6.9
Jamaica (1996)	–	107	–	8.1
Kenya (1995)	–	85	24	–
Kiribati	–	–	–	–
Lesotho (1996)	–	97	29	2.4
Malawi (1995)	–	135	16	0.6
Malaysia (1996)	–	91	62	–
Maldives (1997)	61	125	–	–
Malta (1996)	106	110	–	–

Mauritius (1996)	83	107	65	6.5
Mozambique (1995)	–	60	7	0.4
Namibia (1996)	–	131	61	–
Nauru	–	–	–	–
New Zealand (1996)	77	103	120	58.5
Nigeria (1994)	–	89	30	–
Pakistan (1993)	–	74	–	–
Papua New Guinea (1995)	1	80	14	3.2
St Kitts and Nevis	–	–	–	–
St Lucia	–	–	–	–
Samoa (1994)	–	107	–	–
Seychelles	–	–	–	–
Sierra Leone (1990)	–	50	17	1.3
Singapore (1996)	–	94	72	38.5
Solomon Islands (1994)	36	97	17	–
South Africa (1996)	31	116	84	–
Sri Lanka (1996)	–	109	–	–
Swaziland (1996)	–	129	52	6.0
Tanzania (1996)	–	66	5	–
Tonga	–	–	–	–
Trinidad and Tobago (1995)	–	96	72	7.8
Tuvalu	–	–	–	–
Uganda (1995)	–	73	12	1.7
Vanuatu (1992)	35	106	20	–
Zambia (1995)	–	89	–	–
Zimbabwe (1996)	–	113	48	6.5

Note: 1 Blank fields are due to unavailability of data.
2 Years in parenthesis represent the latest years in which the respective figures were collected.

Source: Compiled from the 1998 UNESCO *Statistical Yearbook*.

Table 2.2 Net Enrolment Ratios for Some Commonwealth Countries, by Level

Countries	First level	Second level
Australia (1996)[1]	97	92
The Bahamas (1993)	95	87
Bangladesh (1990)	62	20
Barbados (1991, 1989)	78	75
Belize (1994, 1992)	99	36
Botswana (1996, 1995)	84	45
Britain (1995)	100	92
Brunei Darussalam (1994)	91	68
Canada (1994, 1995)	95	93
Cyprus (1995)	96	93
Fiji (1992)	99	_2
The Gambia (1995)	65	–
Guyana (1995, 1990)	87	71
Jamaica (1990)	100	62
Lesotho (1996)	63	17
Malawi (1994)	100	–
Malaysia (1994)	91	–
Malta (1996, 95)	100	84
Mauritius (1996)	98	–
Mozambique (1995)	40	6
Namibia (1996)	91	36
New Zealand (1996)	100	97
Samoa (1996)	97	–
Singapore (1995)	94	–
South Africa (1996)	94	51
Sri Lanka	109	–
Swaziland (1996)	95	37
Tanzania (1996)	48	–
Trinidad & Tobago (1995, 1992)	88	64
Vanuatu (1991)	–	17
Zambia (1995, 1994)	75	16

Note: 1 Years in parenthesis represent the latest years in which the respective figures were collected.
2 Blank fields are due to unavailability of data.

Source: Compiled from the 1998 UNESCO *Statistical Yearbook*.

Why Equity is a Critical Adjunct

Education as a social good cannot be discussed independently of equity concerns. To the extent that it is financed and supported by public resources, questions arise about costs and benefits in relation to individuals, groups and society in general. Equity is so important that it is a root cause of much social unrest and disruption in many countries. Ironically, the more a country succeeds with access, the more glaring and intolerable is the problem of equity. When 40 per cent or less of the eligible age group is enrolled in schools, access is a very serious problem. Equity is not necessarily a big issue, especially if access is limited by lack of resources, rather than by any form of discrimination or exclusion. However, when 90 per cent or more of the age group is enrolled in schools, equity becomes a serious and intense problem because of the relative deprivation of the 10 per cent not in school. Who are these people and why are they not in school when almost everyone else has access to education? This is the sense in which access and equity start to become more widely regarded as matters of fundamental human right.

The Typical Barriers to Access

In the conventional, formal school system, access is limited by various factors including:

- *Specific location:* There is usually a building or some form of sheltered area that is designated as a school. Learners, teachers and the resources needed are brought together in the school for learning to take place. This raises problems of distance to school for those who live far away or in difficult areas. Small children may be particularly disadvantaged in this regard if they have to walk long distances to the school. Allied to distance is the issue of safety in making the daily trip to school. In some areas this is a problem particularly for girls, but it is a general consideration which influences uptake of opportunities for education. Yet another factor related to the specific location of schools is the opportunity cost to families. If learners have to travel daily to a specific location to attend school, then they are not available at home to perform essential tasks. This can be a problem where the learners normally make a vital contribution to housework or income-related activities for the family. Such opportunity costs may be too high for some families, resulting in failure to make use of schooling provision. Another factor that influences the uptake of schooling opportunities is the condition of the building or facility that serves as a school. Some of these may pose health risks if they are of poor quality and lack such basics as water and toilets.
- *Standardised provisions:* In the interest of basic quality there are usually some standard specifications for schools, in terms of classrooms, furniture, equipment and learning materials. This makes it difficult for some countries to provide schools in all areas, since neither the government nor the local communities can afford enough of the standard provisions to provide for the education of all their people.
- *Specific times:* Formal school is organised according to specific times which add up to school periods, days, terms and years. In many developing countries of the Commonwealth, this raises problems of opportunity costs for some groups as regards important seasons for economic activities (fishing, harvest, etc.). There is a rhythm to schooling created by its time-specific nature, and those who cannot fit in with this rhythm tend to drop out sooner or later.

- *Specialist staff*: Formal schools require trained teachers and other staff. This means that in some areas it is difficult to start schools due to lack of specialist staff. This requirement can also pose a threat to the viability of schools in remote and sparsely populated regions, where it may not be economical to assign one teacher to each grade due to the small number of total learners. In some cases rural areas may also be unattractive to qualified teachers if there is no adequate housing.
- *Programmed activities*: The formal school operates on a curriculum in which prescribed learning activities are programmed according to a timetable. Where the prescribed learning activities do not appear to have much relevance to local needs, parents may not be inclined to send their children to school. Lack of flexibility means that those who are frequently absent miss much of what is prescribed and eventually tend to drop out of school.
- *Prescribed age groups*: Because learners are organised into age-related classes and each cohort is expected to progress through the system together, there is a tendency for over-aged learners to drop out of school. Also, wastage of school places often occurs due to repetition and over-aged learners.

These and other similar factors also have critical implications for the issue of equity in the provision, distribution and up-take of opportunities for education.

The Factors Affecting Equitable Access to Education

Political ideology and economic policies set the framework within which issues of equity in education are determined. However, tradition and convention can also play a major role, especially in situations where conscious efforts are not made to question and change established practices in the interest of equity. For historical reasons certain population groups have not had the same degree of access to education as the rest of society. In Commonwealth countries, for example, the introduction and growth of modern education was closely associated with the spread of Christianity; other religious groups, or groups strongly opposed to Christianity, lost out on educational opportunities. Similarly, it is often argued that traditional values in many countries regarding the place of females in the family and in society, are partly to blame for persistent low female access to education. Whatever the reasons, there must be deliberate and determined efforts to help address these broad political, socio-economic and cultural issues, in order to ensure greater equity in access to education.

This is not purely a matter of legislation, although it does make a big difference if the laws of the country provide for freedom of access to educational opportunities. The problem is that countries can always use such legislation to claim that access to education is available on an equitable basis for all groups in society. Legislation without further action can be a smoke-screen for retaining privileges and perpetuating the old inequities. For instance, poor groups cannot overcome economic barriers to access by themselves. They invariably need targeted subsidies to meet the direct cost of schooling and flexible arrangements to address the opportunity costs of dealing with income-generating activities while attending school.

All too often the arrangements for education are inflexible and contribute to preventing equitable access. These factors are summarised in Table 2.3 (page 34).

Table 2.3 Educational Factors and Issues Affecting Access and Equity

Conventional factors	Issues relating to access	Issues relating to equity
Specific location Typically a school building that is purpose-built, or adapted for the purpose, is designated as the place where education happens.	• Physical distance to school • Safety of journey to school • Quality of school building • Quality of location • Cost of going to school • Inefficient use of facilities	• Isolated population groups • Nomadic populations • Opportunity costs for poor • Inferior facilities for some • Rural locations unattractive • Could be unsafe for girls
Standardised provision Schools are usually defined in terms of classrooms, furniture, equipment and materials used for teaching and learning.	• High costs so fewer schools• • Non-recognition by officials • Over-crowded schools in high density areas	• Sub-standard provision • Cost burden on the poor • No schools in some areas
Designated time blocks Teaching and learning tend to be organised into time blocks designated for specific activities. Periods, school days, terms and years dominate.	• Clash with other priorities • Needs attendance rhythm • Excludes other activities	• Loss of income for poor • Girls' housework pressure • High opportunity cost
Prescribed age-groups Learners are organised by age into classes or stages. Cohorts of learners are expected to flow through the stages together.	• Lack of full school range • Repeaters tend to drop out • No teachers for all grades	• Over-aged mainly poor • Weak control over learning • Older Girls drop out
Programmed activities Education structured in terms of a prescribed curriculum in the form of a programme of learning/teaching activities.	• Lack of relevance to needs • Alienating content • Absentees lose out	• Cultural disadvantages • Lack of home support
Specialist staff Education is the responsibility of specialist professional staff (teachers, etc.) who should be specially trained for the job.	• Shortage of teachers • No local teachers • High pupil/teacher ratio • High salary budget	• Many unqualified teachers • Poor learning achievement • Lack of role models for the disadvantaged groups

Overview of Current Practices

Over the years most countries have achieved some success in addressing the problem of access to education. Generally the emphasis has been on expansion and innovative use of the formal system. Increased social demand for education has led to a rise in innovative measures, in addition to the straightforward expansion of the formal system. Clearly there was an unwritten and underlying assumption that, given sufficient time and effort, the formal system could cope with the growing demand for education. The range of significant policies and strategies that have played a part in the successful expansion and innovative adaptation of the formal system over the years include:

- use of school mapping to ensure that location and distribution of schools match the population distribution pattern;
- use of multiple shift systems to promote greater enrolment for the same number of educational facilities;
- large class sizes that maximise use of existing facilities;
- multi-grade teaching arrangements that enable schools in remote areas with sparse population to remain viable;
- economies of scale achieved through amalgamation of several small schools that are close to each other, but are owned and/or operated by different agencies;
- provision of school bus services to tackle problems of distance and safety on the journey to school for a wide catchment population of learners;
- use of split-site schools to ensure a division that encourages access – for instance, a school may be split into a girls' school and a boys' school component, with each in a different location; similarly where there is pressure on land and facilities, a school may be spread across several locations in a crowded urban area;
- provision of boarding facilities to ease the burden of daily travel to school for learners spread over a wide catchment area, or those from nomadic populations;
- use of the 'feeder schools' concept to provide schooling closer to home for small children during the first three or four grades. These schools are typically small and limited in their range of provision, but they are close to the learners and involve only minimal travel or safety risks in the journey to school. When the learners have completed the three or four grades in these small schools they can transfer to larger schools that take in students from a number of small schools within a catchment area. Thus learners move from their feeder schools into the large school when they are old enough to make the daily journey to school.

The Rise of Non-Formal Alternatives to the School

It has taken a long time, but the old assumption that the formal system will ultimately be able to cope with increased social demand for schooling, is now being seriously questioned in many countries. Against the background of persistent constraints and problems of formal schooling, efforts have been made in these countries to develop alternative provision. The main problem is that such provision is invariably a response to lack of access to the formal system, rather than a bold new initiative that sets out to offer something different. Such efforts often take the form of development initiatives by community groups and NGOs, in which education is seen as having an important role. In such initiatives it is not always possible to work within the many constraints of the formal education system. On the positive side, the success of these initiatives has often led to governments providing support and taking further action to boost alternative provisions. Examples of alternatives include:

- use of mobile classrooms to serve nomadic and pastoral populations;
- introduction of flexi-schooling arrangements to cater for working youth;
- adult and non-formal education;
- distance learning programmes to reach isolated populations;
- open and more flexible learning systems to match learners' circumstances; and
- community schools that serve multiple development purposes.

Over the years developments in technology have contributed to a range of strategies and practices that have helped to overcome some of the barriers to access and equity in education. In this regard it is very important for countries to take stock of, and appreciate the amount of progress that has been made in this area. However, there is no room for complacency, for problems of access and equity are still of paramount importance in education. It is generally agreed that in many ways formal education has been pushed to the limits in terms of access, through such measures as multiple-shift schools, large class sizes, mobile schools and school mapping. Yet substantial population groups still do not have adequate access to education. Escalating demographic pressures; changing lifestyles; increased expectations; the explosion in knowledge and information; greater democratisation and emphasis on individual and community rights have all contributed to the persistence of these problems. A critical paradox that needs to be appreciated by decision-makers is that success in access can accentuate the problem of equity.

Against this background, it has been suggested that what is needed is a fundamental rethinking on the structure and pattern of organisation that have dominated the formal education system for so long. There is a particularly strong feeling that, with recent advances in technology, education no longer has to be constrained in this way. Increasingly, it is possible to extend access to those outside the education system, and to ensure that those within the system are given greater access to an ever-expanding world of information and knowledge. This is a critical point for decision-makers to appreciate. In terms of equity it implies that even as countries strive to provide for those deprived of educational opportunities, they must also ensure that those who already have access to education are not deprived of access to the wealth of information and knowledge that is now available outside the school. This obviously raises some very fundamental dilemmas in terms of equity. It involves reaching the un-reached, while at the same time enriching the reached. Herein lies the great attraction, as well as the great challenge, of distance education.

Distance education is an area in which technology makes an important impact on access to education. In trying to gain a better understanding of distance education, it is worth remembering that the concept is a very old one. What has changed over the years is the range of technologies and what these have made possible in the field of distance education. It is also worth remembering that distance education is not only about reaching those outside the formal system, but also about enriching what is available to those within it. It is equally important to recognise that the technologies involved in distance learning are simply tools, and not the essence of education. Over the years these tools have revolutionised the ways in which we can generate, package, disseminate, store, retrieve and utilise knowledge and information (Table 2.4, page 39). In other words, such tools provide us with an enhanced mechanism for delivering education.

Yet we must not overlook the enduring nature of 'old technology' despite the emergence of 'new technology' in this field. For instance, printing is one of the oldest technologies available, and printed materials are still the most widely used media in standard classrooms as well as in distance learning programmes. The most critical element in any distance learning programme is not so much the technology used to deliver programmes, but the degree to which the materials are *self-instructional* for the target group. Decision-makers need to guard against the dangers of 'fadism' or hankering after the latest technology just to be in fashion. There is a constant tension between embracing new technology and getting old technology to work more efficiently for the education system. This is often mediated by cost considerations as well as by constraints in current capacity as far as the needs of the new technologies are concerned.

At the tertiary level, distance education is currently one of the fastest growing fields. Its potential is being rapidly exploited to open up access to tertiary education for the great majority of learners who cannot participate through the conventional route. There is also a growing trend in tertiary education of dual institutions, which offer some form of distance education courses in addition to their conventional programmes. In some cases, there is still a preference for separate distance learning institutions, such as the University of South Africa (UNISA) in South Africa, and Open Universities in Tanzania and Zimbabwe, for example. We must not forget that universities have always conducted some form of distance learning programmes, as for instance with their outreach courses and extra-mural studies programmes. What is new is the more systematic and sustained effort to provide university education to a wider population through distance learning. It is increasingly common for people to gain higher education through distance learning while doing other things in life. Higher education is potentially accessible to a much wider range of people than full-time resident university students.

Within the Commonwealth regional universities have been set up to serve a number of small states where it would not be feasible for each to have a university of its own. Prime examples are the University of the West Indies (UWI) and the University of the South Pacific (USP). Both make extensive use of distance learning methodologies for delivering their programmes. In addition to these regional universities, there are a growing number of national open universities in the Commonwealth, which have developed a strong reputation for effective use of distance education to reach a wide student population. Amongst the best known are the Indira Ghandi Open University of India, the Allama Iqbal Open University of Pakistan and UNISA.

Another significant factor in the rise of distance education is the decline in funding for higher education in some Commonwealth countries, which has eroded capacity and standards over the years. This has led to a situation in which higher education institutions, particularly in Africa, are now seeking to make use of external inputs through the modern technologies that promote distance learning at a more interactive level. One of the most promising examples of this is in the African Virtual University (AVU) initiative which is being piloted in several countries with support from the World Bank. The case study from Kenya (page 51) gives a fascinating insight into progress of this initiative. Yet another important source of pressure to link up with external institutions is the increase in franchising efforts by universities in the developed Commonwealth, as part of their income-generating strategy. This pressure is targeted mainly at the newly industrialised Commonwealth countries as well as the richer small states of the Commonwealth. In both cases there is a large potential for courses leading to overseas qualifications, and franchising makes it cheaper to obtain such qualifications locally.

In addition to the growth of distance education at the tertiary level, there is a growing desire to use it for the delivery of secondary education. While there are examples of successful adaptation of secondary curriculum for adult learners through distance learning (for example in South Africa), this is a much more challenging proposition. The main problem is that distance learning presupposes that learners are highly motivated; have adequate language skills and proficiency, and have some familiarity with whatever technology is being used (audio/video tapes, computers, etc.). Unfortunately, this is far from the case for the average secondary-aged learner in many Commonwealth countries, whether developing or developed. At this age most learners are not yet capable of working largely on their own with minimum supervision. The primary education system does not prepare them for this. It is therefore difficult to use distance education for delivery of the secondary curriculum to students who have just completed primary education. This is not to say that some countries have not attempted to do so in the past. The demise of the Distance Education Centres (DECs) in Malawi bears testimony to the difficulties involved and the unfortunate consequences that can result from such efforts. Hopefully, important lessons can be learned from such attempts. It remains to be seen whether current efforts and investments in secondary distance education in Mozambique will be more successful. In reality, there are no really successful examples of using distance education at secondary level in Commonwealth countries. We may have to await a new kind of primary or basic education which better prepares learners for self learning, before distance secondary education becomes truly feasible.

In general terms, however, distance learning has become increasingly significant as a means of delivering educational programmes for several reasons:

· the exponential expansion in knowledge and information over the years has meant that the walls of formal institutions can no longer contain most of what needs to be learned. Equally, teachers are becoming less purveyors of knowledge and more managers of the learning process. It is therefore inevitable that at various times and for various purposes, learners need to look beyond the formal institution for sources of knowledge and information;
· distance learning methodologies help to promote equity in many situations where formal institutions are very unequally resourced in terms of trained teachers. Through distance education it is possible to use the best teachers to deliver a range of well-planned lessons to all institutions;
· through the use of self-instructional materials, it is possible to conduct teacher training by distance education courses. This has the potential of reducing the cost of teacher training quite dramatically, as well as expanding access to training courses for many more serving teachers who need training;
· individuals for whom conventional education programmes are not suitable can pursue tertiary and even secondary programmes through distance education. Courses can be pursued by people who are in full-time employment, or who are doing other things like taking care of their families.

Despite the growing importance of distance education, it would be wrong to regard it as yet another panacea for the problems of equitable access in education. Certainly it is one of the mechanisms for expanding access, and in certain circumstances it can help to deal with the problem of equity. In the main, however, countries will have to address the much more fundamental questions of re-allocating educational resources and providing targeted subsidies, as well as designing interventions to help groups overcome the various barriers to equitable access in education. When considering the use of technology to promote equitable access, countries should undertake a basic analysis of the ways in which a wide range of technologies could be useful for generating and packaging knowledge, and for the transmission and dissemination of knowledge in the process of delivering education. These and other related properties of the various technologies will determine their usefulness for equitable access in education (Table 2.4).

Table 2.4 Matrix of Technologies and their Properties

Clusters of education-related technology (by level)	Generating and packaging of knowledge and information	Transmission and dissemination of knowledge and information	Storage and retrieval of knowledge and information	Pattern of use and level of accessibility
Level 1 Face-to-face; spoken word;	• Time-bound • Place-bound • Interactive	• Very highly restricted • Unreliable • Gossip and rumour	• Restricted • Fallible • Memory	• Very highly interactive • Low access
Level 2 Manual writing; typewriting	• Place-bound • Not usually interactive • Low level of efficiency	• Usually slow • Reliable • High costs	• Easy to store • Reliable • Recordable • Retrievable	• Reference • Modest level of access • Low level of interaction
Level 3 Printing; photocopying;	• Place-bound • Not usually interactive • Modest level of efficiency	• Usually slow • Reliable • Lower cost	• Easy to store • Reliable • Recordable • Retrievable	• Reference • Good access • Low level of interaction
Level 4 Radio; television;	• Can break time barriers • Can break place barrier • Can be interactive	• Fast/instant • Reliable • Lower cost	• Recordable • Reliable • Retrievable	• High level of access • Good source of news
Level 5 Telephone; fax machine	• Break time and place barriers • Interactive	• Fast/instant • Reliable • High cost	• Reliable • Recordable • Retrievable	• Good access • Good level of interaction
Level 6 Audio/video recording;	• Independent of time and place	• Reliable • High cost	• Reliable • Retrievable • Excellent for storage	• Reference • Source of news • Fair access
Level 7 Computer; electronic mail; www/internet; video conferencing	• Break time and place barriers • Interactive	• Fast/instant • Reliable • High cost	• High storage cost • Easy to store • Recordable • Retrievable	• High level of access • Very highly interactive • Reference • Source of news

Addressing the Challenges

Some of the critical challenges facing governments concerning the use of technology in access to education may be summarised as follows:

· meeting the costs of current provisions and making the investments necessary to extend such provision to reach those excluded to date (sustainability);
· making full and efficient use of existing and old technologies where it is more cost effective or appropriate to do so;
· promoting diversity of educational provision to break down barriers by moving away from the 'one-size-fits-all' notion of formal education.
· restructuring educational financing to reflect a more holistic approach to formal and non-formal provision; maximise equitable access, and promote equality of outcomes.

All governments have to face the major challenge of finding extra resources to meet the need for equitable expansion of education in a manner that is sustainable in the long term. This need goes beyond the capital cost of constructing, furnishing and equipping new classrooms. It involves the short-term cost of training additional teachers for the expanded system, and various other capital costs. However, it is in the area of recurrent costs that governments face the greatest challenge. In many countries the education recurrent budget mainly covers staff salaries, leaving little for pedagogical items.

Often the challenge is to find more efficient ways of spending current resources, and to search for new money to increase the level of the recurrent budget available for education. These two aspects of the challenge are closely inter-related. Ministries of Education need to show that they are using existing resources in the most efficient manner possible before additional resources can be justified for the education system. Conversely, putting additional resources into a very inefficient system is simply wasteful.

In the quest for efficiency the challenges faced by governments include the removal of hidden subsidies that benefit powerful groups in society, and the need to change long-established but inefficient practices and patterns that may have been wrongly associated with 'quality education'. Countries will need to persuade and campaign for this kind of change in education. Change can easily be derailed by powerful interest groups if they are not persuaded to see and appreciate what is in the best interest of the population in general and the nation as a whole. These are sensitive issues and countries need external support to deal with them in a responsible manner.

One of the main challenges relating to new resources is the debt burden faced by many countries. Servicing and repayment of external debts leaves little or no additional resources for investing in sectors like education and health. Developments in the area of debt relief now offer great hope that the highly indebted poor countries (HIPCs) will have substantial resources to channel into education and health.

Formulating Policies and Strategies

It is important for governments to embark on well thought out policies and to engage in feasible strategies to address the question of technology and access to education. These should provide answers to such questions as:

- Who is entitled to participate in the existing education provisions?
- Are specific groups or communities excluded by definition from participating in these provisions?
- Are current provisions adequate to meet the general demand for education?
- Are there problems on the demand side in terms of poor up-take of opportunities provided for basic education?
- What are the main obstacles to education for all?
- How can we best reach those who are not being reached by current provisions?
- What is the trade-off between expanded access and quality of education?

If governments are to meet the demand for equitable access to education, they need to move increasingly towards encouraging a diversity of provision from formal schooling monopolies to a wide range of alternative opportunities and provisions. If these alternatives are to be credible, they must be designed and funded to function as more than 'second rate and last resort' options for those who cannot gain access to the formal system. It is critical that measures are taken to ensure equity of outcomes. Learners may take different routes in terms of access to education, but they should be guaranteed similar outcomes in terms of the learning achievements possible and available to them. This is feasible in principle, but in reality major problems of perception and attitude make it difficult to equate alternative provisions with the main-stream formal education system. These problems impact very strongly on the equity issue, in terms of who has access to what. Almost without exception, the alternative provisions lauded in the literature are targeted at the poor, the disadvantaged and those who for other reasons do not have access to formal, main-stream education. Hence the perception that all forms of alternative provision are inferior and should not be trusted to deliver good quality education. That is why countries must bridge the gap between formal and non-formal education provision, and develop a holistic system that embraces both kinds of provision. This is not a simple challenge, for it would require constructive collaboration between NGOs, community organisations, private providers and governments.

In order to begin to address the many complex issues relating to this notion of equity of outcomes, governments should embark on genuine partnerships with other education providers to:

- develop improved linkages and articulation between the various forms of educational provision;
- work towards a more integrated approach to the provision of educational opportunities, so that learners can have greater flexibility and genuine choice; and
- develop a system for dealing with the management of this integrated diversity of educational provision.

In situations where equity is affected by the exclusion of certain groups from mainstream education, it is important that governments take special measures to tackle the problem. For instance, in a number of Commonwealth African countries the problem of providing education for nomadic populations has entailed the use of special measures such as mobile schools and flexible schedules for schooling.

Perhaps the most important area for policies and strategies to impact on equitable access is in the re-allocation of resources. Even the poorest countries currently spend a significant proportion of government budget and GDP on education. This fact, more than anything else, suggests that the solution to the problem of equitable access is not fundamentally one of new resources. Political decisions need to be made about who should pay what for education, in a manner that would allow governments to use existing resources to promote equitable access as one of their main objectives. Already the indications are that choices have to be made between levels of education, kinds of education and groups of learners. Support for basic education for all is one of the commitments that most governments have made since the World Conference on Education for All at Jomtien in 1990. Even so, blanket subsidies implied in declarations of free basic education cannot be fully justified. Governments need to be more selective in targeting subsidies to those most in need and who face the greatest obstacles in terms of access to basic education. At secondary and higher levels of education the argument for subsidies is even more complex. In essence, subsidies should be used mainly to support and give leverage to the government's education policies and strategies. The same is true of technical and vocational education and other kinds of employment-related training. The key issue is partnership between governments, the private sector, NGOs, local communities and beneficiaries of the educational provision in society.

Clearly there is no simple technology fix that can address the critical issues related to equitable access to education. There are complex considerations which require well-thought-out policies, carefully designed strategies and bold measures in implementation. Technology has a role to play, but it should not be considered in isolation as some sort of *deus ex machina*!

Case Study 1: Closing the Gap Between Information Rich and Poor in South African Schools

Professor Roy Williams
Education for Development, Reading University, UK

Introduction

The impact of new technologies is exciting as well as a cause for concern. The pessimists say that new technologies 'always tend to increase differences in power and access to facilities', and that is often the case. ICT (Information and Communication Technology) has enormous potential to assist in development and, in particular, in the provision of schooling and education. We are told that we should all be moving into an *information society*, composed of *learning organisations*, connected to a *world-wide network of global e-mail and e-commerce and instant international web-based information*.

Various countries have made a commitment to the information society, as well as to equity in education. The President of South Africa, Thabo Mbeki, first made a commitment to developing ICT in 1996 at the G7 (Group of Seven Developed Countries) Conference held in Johannesburg, and the South African Constitution guarantees the equivalent of ten years of free schooling to both adults and children. The Prime Minister of the UK, Tony Blair, has made commitments to ICT across the economy, and his Department for International Development (DfID) has reformulated its policy goals in terms of a radical reduction in poverty.

The question is whether these two objectives can be reconciled. This study will examine various processes in ICT policy and implementation in South Africa, and the way in which the potential for schooling can be realised. This is relevant not only to South Africa, but also to a number of other countries. Many of the issues arise out of my own experience and involvement in these processes, and some of them form the basis for ongoing project design and project work.

Education and Poverty

Oxfam has recently published figures which show that increasing access to education has a direct correlation with development – in health, agriculture and business. There are two related concerns in terms of the relationship between education, poverty and ICT: first, what exactly does ICT have to offer to education – particularly to schools that have so many other problems in other areas? Second, how can poorly resourced schools benefit from ICT, without losing all their best teachers and pupils to rich metropolitan schools? In other words, will the introduction of ICT in poorly resourced schools simply mean that the best people in those schools are creamed off into the cities, leaving the schools increasingly poorer in human resources, and more marginalised within the economy?

Policy Developments in South Africa

In November 1995, the South African Ministry of Education held a national workshop on what it termed 'technology enhanced learning'. This term was formulated very deliberately to prioritise learning, and to ensure that technology served learning, and not vice versa.

In 1996 a team of consultants and stakeholders, from South Africa as well as from several other countries, met over a period of three months to research and produce a proposal for Technology Enhanced Learning (TELI) for the Minister of Education. The team decided that there was no uniform 'learning environment' in South Africa, for which a uniform and standardised set of recommendations could be determined. And on evaluating a number of case studies in South Africa, it became clear that the application of ICT and other technologies to enhance learning varied, and had to vary, from context to context, depending on the particular need that had to be addressed.

Consequently the discussion paper prepared for the Minister took on a unique form: it developed a decision-making framework for educators, rather than a set of recommendations for bureaucrats. It started with analyses of trends in education, technology and development. It stated quite clearly that there was no way in which the current best practices in South African education could be multiplied and made available to all – the numbers did not add up, and they will not in future either.

This means, first, that if equity and quality in education are to be achieved, the new economies of scale of the new technologies will have to be used. Second, the fact that the 'learning environment' – quite simply those places, facilities and people who enable learning to take place – is expanding rapidly beyond the school walls should be welcomed and not resisted. For it is only by harnessing and co-ordinating the varied resources inside and outside of the school walls that education for all will be attainable. The education sector alone will not have the resources to do it. Third, it is the enduring human resource – the teachers – who must be supported first and foremost. Of course learners must have access to the best tools and techniques to enhance their learning. But the teachers must remain central to learning: they must be ahead of the learners, which means that they must become learners too – both in terms of mastering the technology, and in terms of welcoming the opportunities to learn from rapidly developing world-wide information resources. And they must embrace the new 'flatter', non-hierarchical relationships to knowledge and expertise.

After completing the analyses of trends in learning, technology and development, the TELI team developed a decision-making framework, which consists of four parts, all of which are essential to good decisions about TELI, but which can be approached in any order. This is a departure from previous approaches to decision-making, and to the management of educational resources.

Its most important feature is that it is a decision-making process which *depends on the context*, and within that context, on learning needs and goals; existing resources and skills; levels of professional and technical support available, and competing claims for resources. In short, it proposes 'contingency based' decision-making. Another way of putting this is that 'administering standardised procedures' has been replaced by 'managing contingent needs and priorities'. This requires no less than *a change in the organisational culture of education*: from the 'bureaucratic administration' of the past, which was the basis of the *modernist* 'civil service', to a more *post-modernist* 'executive management' that is now required, and which in the past was exclusive to the private sector. What this means is that people in Education will have to learn to make *different decisions within the same framework* – a far cry from the days when all you had to do was to carry out the same directives from the Department of Education in the same way.

After the Minister of Education published the TELI report, a number of public consultations were held in late 1996 and early 1997. The Ministry then set up a second phase, charged with producing a strategic plan for the country. This was done, and some overall programme and financial planning was tabled in 1997. It prioritised

· curriculum development in three key areas in Grade 8;
· delivering technical education in three priority areas;
· developing generic ICT literacy courses;
· professional development of educators;
· training and support of managers;
· pilot projects to test the new approach.

This was a mixed blessing. On the one hand, it included pilot projects to test the new approach, and training and support for managers, who needed to make no less than a cultural shift to implement it. It also included some of the generic resources, such as ICT literacy, which are necessary in any situation of this kind.

On the other hand, by prioritising six large, nationally targeted, undifferentiated mass application programmes, it was in danger of defaulting back to the strengths of the past – large, standardised applications – rather than grasping the challenge of the future, in which not only the *learning environment* but also the *educational management environment* will be characterised by far less certainty, and will require many more on-the-spot, contextually-determined applications. There is, of course, a middle way, in which a multi-faceted and flexible approach, *resource-based learning*, can be used within nationally targeted development areas. It remains to be seen which approach is adopted.

At the same time, the Telecommunications and Broadcasting sectors (in one Ministry), the vocational training sector (in another Ministry: Labour), and a number of initiatives in ICT in yet another Ministry (Arts and Culture), as well as the State broadcaster SABC (South African Broadcasting Corporation), were being developed. With the exception of a joint initiative between the SABC and the Ministry of Education, they were not co-ordinated to any substantial extent. In addition, many of the large educational institutions in the State sector – mainly tertiary education institutions such as the national distance education institutions UNISA (University of South Africa) and TSA (Technikon South Africa), as well as some of the residential universities – were all establishing their own learning support centres, as was the Universal Service Agency in the Ministry of Telecommunications (but attached to the Telecoms regulator, SATRA).

Clearly a great deal of activity is taking place. However, without real co-ordination in the State sector (to say nothing of private initiatives such as M-WEB within the M-NET broadcasting company), the more ICT is developed for learning, the more it might lead to duplication and inefficiency, in everyone's rush to get on board first.

The issue is not amenable to easy solutions. The several State Ministries and semi-autonomous institutions all have their own separate targets and goals to pursue. And although much money is spent on the nine Provincial administrations and legislatures, they do not have any authority over many of the activities of the national institutions in their provinces. The situation is very different from the kind of services offered by Posts and/or Telecommunications in the past, in which the service and the service providers were unified in one 'PTT' (Post and Telecommunications Territory), and in which they held a total monopoly on services.

Nowadays there are several networks – land-line telephones, cell phones, satellite and broadcasting communications, and a vast mix of service providers – each with their own lines of responsibility. The sector is starting to look as if it is regulated by 'market'-type forces, rather than by public policy and public service, but at the moment it looks like neither the one nor the other. However, there is neither the desire nor the political will to move education into a 'regulated–partly privatised' sector, as has happened in broadcasting and telecommunications. The South African paper at the G7 Conference in 1996 provided the framework, but not the detail, for an overall approach to ICT development, although it has not yet resulted in a co-ordinated approach. The South African position paper at that conference identified the priorities as:

- centres of excellence to develop applications;
- multi-purpose community centres for universal access;
- Government-online;
- a national IT qualifications framework; and
- a contemporary music and arts archive.

The TELI initiative has subsequently been expanded in policy terms to include Southern Africa, and the first TELISA centre was established in late 1998 in Maseru, Lesotho.

Developments in Education

During this time a number of initiatives have taken place in schools. The Western Cape Schools Net has been extrapolated to the SA (South African) Schools Net, to expand access to the network. The Canadians (IDRC – International Development Research Centre) have been working throughout the period covered in this study (1994–8) to assist in building facilities in Africa for development, including education. The World Bank has been giving support to the Soweto Technology Project since 1997. The best network, UNINET, has been developed for the tertiary education sector, based at the Foundation for Research Development in Pretoria. This could be expanded for all education. There is also a very promising pilot project which is using a 'CIDS' 2 Megahertz two-way microwave link between St Albans School and Mamelodi Education Centre in Pretoria.

Associated with a project to develop content for ICT applications in education, under the auspices of the Telematics for African Development, a group of people formed the Schools Hypermedia Working Group, and met during 1997 and 1998 to exchange ideas and develop best practices.

Several issues arose out of this work, which have general relevance for educational applications and development of ICT. Many South African schools are poorly resourced – many lack just about everything, from running water and sewage facilities upwards. But they also lack educational materials – textbooks and resource materials for learning. This is partly because the new 'outcomes-based' approach is premised on using a variety of resources, and partly because the transition from apartheid education, in particular the deployment of teachers, was badly handled. Teachers were offered voluntary redundancy, and many of the best teachers took the offer from the State, and moved to the rapidly growing private sector, in which many schools are starting to offer foreign-accredited courses. As a result, the Education Department had to cut back on funds for textbooks, and publishers reduced their staff by up to 50 per cent in 1998.

However, there are ways in which ICT can be used in poorly resourced schools which strengthen those schools; provide learning and professional opportunities for teachers; improve education for the pupils; provide some economic opportunities for the schools and their communities, and make resource materials available which are appropriate for the context and culture of that community.

There are several broad considerations. Most important is that the exercise of providing ICT support to enhance learning must be both conservative and radical at the same time. This might sound strange, but it is important to understand these issues.

During apartheid, and particularly in the 1980s, a very strong 'progressive' education sector developed – much of it feeding into the NEPI (National Education Policy Initiative) and the policy and planning that followed during and after the first democratic election. Many people within the progressive sector of education feel very strongly that only the best, most progressive methodologies must be supported. This makes sense at one level. But it does not take account of the fact that however much effort is put into upgrading teachers, it will take a long time – years and years – and in the meantime teachers have to get on with providing learning opportunities for their pupils. In practical terms, this means that teachers must, first, be supported in what they are already doing. And if that means getting them better notes to write on the blackboard, for everyone to copy down, day after day, and calling it teaching, then that is a start. It would also demonstrate to teachers that the notion that TELI supports their needs can be taken at face value, and it would give them immediate value added, which is recognisably theirs.

The notes that teachers currently use can be upgraded by e-mailing them to a 'moderation and editing' centre, where they can be improved, and sent back – in the same format in which they arrived (probably A4). Then these same notes can be used as the basis for much more radical developments. They could be the basis for hypertext notes, for multimedia, for student collaboration, and so on. In an ICT world, it does not matter if the same materials are made available in many different versions. Storage is no longer expensive, and schools can choose which versions they want to use and print out.

In this way a number of different formats of materials can be developed, using ideas from outside the school, as well as materials from teachers who know what is appropriate for their learners. The most radical and the most conservative enhancements of learning can, and should, be developed alongside each other. We no longer live in a single-track modernist world, and education can benefit from multiple format resources.

There are a number of more detailed parameters that would allow this to happen:

· *The borders of the school should not be the borders of learning.* Whether teachers, pupils or parents are using ICT resources, the school must not, and cannot any longer, define the borders of learning. Low-cost connections to people, texts, projects and communities must be exploited to the full, and the school should be developed into *one of the best places from which to access learning*, instead of the *only place to go to receive teaching*. Creative ways of doing this without running up exorbitant telephone bills are readily available – various permutations of Web-CDs, intranets, extranets and virtual internets, using a variety of communication technologies to transmit information, can be used.

· *Use a variety of media and resources, and never let particular technologies dictate what you do.* Useful as ICT is, it is not the only game in town, and paper, live interaction, radio, television and tape-recorders will all still have their place. Paper magazines are one of the most popular media in many poor communities, and people's existing media consumption patterns should be capitalised on, not ignored.

· *Teachers rather than pupils need to be the primary beneficiaries.* This does not exclude pupils from using ICT, but it does argue for leverage into education through improving the key and enduring resource in schools – the teachers. It also makes sure that the teachers are valued, and see themselves as valuable resources, instead of feeling threatened and marginalised. In the end teachers will have to ensure that ICT works in schools. We will never get to the point where we will hold individual children solely responsible for their learning – teachers and schools will always be expected to bear overall responsibility.

In most poor communities in the world, and in most poorly resourced schools, it will not be possible for every child to get open access to ICT in the next ten years. However, it is entirely feasible for every teacher to have sufficient and useful access to ICT via teachers' centres – at schools or in other buildings – and to slowly build up access for pupils.

· *Start with familiar practices, proven needs, and existing information flows.* Teachers in all schools have information – texts – which they use in their class-rooms. These are familiar, and are used in familiar ways. The content, design and presentation, and the educational methodology might be less than perfect, but what is important is that they are often phrased in a language, and make use of examples, that speak directly to the pupils in that context and that culture.

· *Improve teachers' own resources and texts, and feed them back quickly to the teachers.* All that is required is to let some of them input their texts into a computer, feed it into an e-mail network, and for someone at a central point to provide an editing and mediation service, and send them out again.

   The mediation part of the centre would provide the human interface so that teachers do not have to spent a lot of time and money browsing the internet – they can be pointed in the right direction, and given advice on what is useful.

   The editing centre would revise these texts, and improve the language, layout and design, add detail and related examples, offer ideas for practical and collaborative work, and links to other resources. A system of portable document formatting (pdf) allows documents to be transported between computers, whatever the platform.

   The texts could then be fed back quickly to the teachers in a such a way that they would:

   – remain recognisably *theirs* – so that they *own* and are proud of the material they have produced, and which others can use;

   – be available in the form with which they are most familiar – probably an A4 print-out, and in *lesson-sized* chunks;

- also be available in web-format, with useful links to many other resources; and
- be made available, in principle, to all other teachers.

• *Establish cost-effective ways of making the resources available.* It would be wonderful if it were possible to give everyone access to the world-wide web, 24 hours a day, but this will remain prohibitively expensive to most poor communities for years to come. However, there are ways to get around telephone line costs: from sending updates on CD-ROM or even diskettes, to using computer network *mirroring techniques.* In this way simulated or virtual access to the information can be provided.

• *Develop cost-effective knowledge bases for learners.* Teachers' notes can be upgraded for teachers. But they can also provide opportunities for students to
- compile and author their own knowledge base of notes and resources, whether in paper or digital form.
- compile their own hypermedia resources, which could be made available to the next class of pupils doing that course.

• *Provide rewards and ownership.* Resources produced by teachers and pupils should be *theirs,* but they should also be available to others. There are ways to define and share copyright, so that everyone in the system benefits. ICT enthusiasts will put extraordinary amounts of effort into developing resources, but they will migrate to commercial publishing houses in the cities very quickly if their time and effort is not recognised.

The school also needs to be able to rearrange duties and responsibilities, and manage a number of new ways in which particular teachers can contribute to ICT-enhanced learning – not only in their school, but in a broader educational setting. Educational management must adjust to these changes, or loose its best resources.

• *Provide economic opportunities for poor communities.* In the early stages, teachers would input texts and receive revised texts. Later on, they could develop editing skills, become part of the editing network, and be paid for it. They could also become *e-mail tutors* for pupils from other schools – this should be a key part of a learning network, and it also requires changes in educational management.

These opportunities can, in a small way, start to provide economic input into poor communities. If the teachers could stay in the communities, and at the same time develop their professional skills and increase their earning power, they would spend some of that money in those poorer areas. It would be possible to draw up project guidelines which require the increasing use of teachers in poor schools for increasingly more responsible jobs in the network.

• *Maximise choice.* One of the most impressive things about ICT is that information resources can be stored and communicated at ever decreasing costs, and this trend will continue for years to come. This means that there does not have to be one way of doing or presenting anything. Many versions of the same lesson, description, report, or text, are possible, and it should not matter which ones the pupils and teachers use. They will have to learn to be more discerning, but that is a useful life-skill to develop anyway.

• *Provide guidance and navigation in resource bases.* The downside of ICT is that it provides even more information in a world which already suffers from information overload. It is possible to provide tracking and guidance within an ICT resource base, which would greatly enhance the user-friendliness of the resources.

For instance, different schools and teachers can tag or mark their texts according to their learners and the contexts in which they find themselves. People using the system will be free to use whatever parts they like, but they could choose to tailor their searches and use of the resources in ways that more closely mirror the profiles of their learners. Customised learning resources are possible – both in the sense of choosing between different sets of materials on the same topic, and in terms of teachers further customising those resources as they become adept at manipulating the information and tools.

Conclusion

In this way, poorly resourced schools can provide learning and professional opportunities for teachers; improve the education available for the pupils; provide some economic opportunities for the schools and their communities, and make available resource materials which are appropriate for the context and culture of particular communities.

These schools can also be part of a much broader collaboration, in which all schools contribute to educational development. This model can be implemented specifically for poorly resourced schools. It can also provide opportunities for all other schools – both to contribute to, and to benefit from, a wide choice of educational ideas, resources, and personal and professional contacts.

There are technical, curriculum, materials development, and broad management issues to be solved. They can be solved, and the investment of time and effort will yield demonstrative benefits.

It is important that people and countries who are thinking of developing ICT resources for schools should understand, and think through, the policy, decision-making and management, cost, and plain usefulness in the classroom of ICT before going ahead. But there is no doubt that 'ICT' is exciting, and offers particular economies of scale and opportunities hitherto unimagined, if only we keep in mind the people who would like it to be useful and easy to use in their day-to-day lives.

Note

There are three main sources of information about ICT in South Africa, each of which has many links to other sites:
1 Sangonet: www.sn.apc.org
2 Africa Internet Connectivity: www3.sn.apc.org/Africa
3 SAIDE (SA Institute for Distance Education): www.SAIDE.org.za, particularly a paper by Neil Butcher (1998): *The possibilities and pitfalls of harnessing ICTs to accelerate social development: a South African perspective*, which is as encyclopaedic as its name, but nevertheless very useful.

Case Study 2: The African Virtual University (AVU) – Kenyatta University, Kenya

Dr Magdallen N. Juma

Director, AVU, Kenyatta University, Nairobi, Kenya

Introduction

African higher education has witnessed unprecedented expansion in the past several decades. Many African countries which had a single university at independence now (1998) have several universities and colleges. With the achievement of independence in the 1960s by most African countries, the rate of expansion has averaged 11 per cent per year for the past 30 years, with enrolment increasing from around 21,000 in 1960 to around 500,000 by the mid 1980s.

Kenya is among the countries that have experienced an explosive growth in university education in the last 20 years or so. From one university (the University of Nairobi) with a student population of 2,786 in 1970, there are now five public universities in Kenya – namely, Nairobi, Kenyatta, Moi, Egerton and Jomo Kenyatta University of Agriculture and Technology. The student enrolment rose to around 40,000 in the 1991–92 academic year. In the 1996–97 academic year, enrolment declined significantly by 5.2 per cent to stand at 37,973 against 40,065 students in the 1995–96 academic year. The drop is explained partly by the gradual graduation of the double intake of students admitted in the 1990–91 academic year, and partly by the inability of some parents to pay college fees (Republic of Kenya, 1997:201).

The rise in student numbers has also meant growth in the teaching staff. The size of the university teaching staff quadrupled from 434 in 1970 to 1,800 in 1989, coinciding with a significant rise in student enrolments during this time. Although the proportion of Kenyans on the academic staff is over 80 per cent, poor remuneration compared with other sectors has resulted in many vacancies and the hiring of less qualified staff. A high proportion of staff are Master's degree holders. Competition for qualified staff among the public universities has also resulted in uneven promotion criteria.

The growth in enrolment is mainly a consequence of the insatiable public demand for higher and higher levels of education, as primary and secondary levels can no longer guarantee modern sector wage employment. Related to this is the nature of Kenya's reward structure which favours those with formal education qualifications who are engaged in wage employment in general and professional employment in particular. However, public demand has been an important factor influencing university growth, mainly because university education has experienced increasing politicisation. Thus the main initial justification for university expansion – the need for the generation of skilled, high-level manpower – has been replaced with a political one in which university expansion is seen more in terms of its political potentials to equalise economic opportunities at both the individual and regional levels (Sifuna, 1997).

With regard to funding, in recent years higher education has been funded more substantially than any other level of education. Higher education's share of the

1992–93 Government allocation, for example, amounted to 19 per cent of the national recurrent budget for education and over 56 per cent of the Government's development budget (funds for building, equipment and other capital investments). National recurrent budget expenditures per student in public universities for 1992–93 were 46 times higher than those for each primary school pupil. In other words, higher education is mainly funded by the Government. Students are required to pay nominal fees, amounting to roughly 10 per cent of the total Government recurrent expenditure for higher education.

Despite the astronomical Government expenditure on higher education, the rapid expansion of university education and increased enrolment have not been accompanied by a commensurate rise in the level of Government funding, to ensure a high quality of instruction. There are therefore serious problems in the public universities related to instructional quality, class sizes and availability of materials and facilities.

This state of affairs prevails in the five public universities, although each of them has its own peculiar problems. For example, enrolment at Kenyatta University went up by 5 per cent to 8,574 students in the 1996–97 academic year. In this period the University enrolled a total of 294 postgraduate students, of whom 133 were pursuing doctoral degrees (Republic of Kenya, 1997:292). These student numbers were not matched with the provision of teaching facilities and resources, especially in Science where laboratories and equipment intended for 30 students were now used by ten times that number. The calibre of the teaching staff did not improve the situation.

Background to the African Virtual University (AVU)

The essential problem confronted by university managers, academic staff, Government policy makers, graduate employers, students and their families is that the quality of university education in Africa has declined significantly. This is true regardless of how quality is defined: student performance on standardised test; academic staff credentials; student exposure to current knowledge and information; relevance of learning to labour market requirements, and academic capacities for development in Africa – on the whole, all have been declining. A significant opportunity is created by AVU to catalyse constructive action in this arena. The AVU model will assist in tapping the potential offered by new technologies to overcome some of the financial, physical and information barriers that prevent increased access to high quality education in Sub-Saharan Africa.

Furthermore, the emergence of the virtual university model presents an exciting opportunity. For instance, the growth of new technologies makes possible the creation of virtual universities where quality professors, libraries and laboratories can be shared by people and organisations in physically unconnected places. The pedagogical advantages afforded by the model of virtual universities are even more significant: they enable the creation of more current programmes of studies and curriculum content at Kenyatta University in fields such as computer science and computer engineering which do not exist as programmes of study in the University. The introduction of short courses – Internet Access; C++ Computer Programming; Computer Architecture and Design; Introduction to Engineering and the virtual seminars add a new dimension in augmenting and supplementing current university programmes. The new courses provided by the AVU model adapt to demand and keep up with the latest advances in disciplines of studies.

Essentially, AVU is a concept or model of distance education that uses a technological mode of instructional delivery. It is the first of its kind – an interactive, instructional telecommunications network – established to serve countries of Sub-Saharan Africa. It is funded by the World Bank, with headquarters in Washington DC. AVU's mission is to use the power of modern information technologies to increase access to educational resources throughout Sub-Saharan Africa. Its objective is to build world-class degree programmes that support economic development by the education and training of world-class scientists, technicians, engineers, business managers, health care providers, and other professionals.

The Implementation and Current Status of AVU

AVU is being developed and implemented in three phases. First, the prototype/pilot phase, which was implemented in 1997–98. The purpose of this phase was to establish partnerships with institutions of higher education throughout Sub-Saharan Africa, in order to offer technology-based credit courses and non-credit seminars using digital-satellite technology.

A successful prototype service phase will provide the foundation for the second phase of AVU, which will include offering complete undergraduate degree programmes from leading universities world-wide, beginning in 1999.

The third phase of AVU will follow with the development and offering of science and technology curricula from one or more partner institutions in Sub-Saharan Africa. The full implementation of the third phase will be resource sharing of technology-based degree programmes among institutions of higher education throughout Sub-Saharan Africa.

For the 1998–99 academic year, the following 27 institutions will offer AVU courses:

- Addis Ababa University, Ethiopia
- Cape Verde Higher Education Institute, Cape Verde
- Egerton University, Kenya
- Kenyatta University, Kenya
- Kigali Institute of Science and Technology, Rwanda
- Loko Vocational School, Ivory Coast
- Makerere University, Uganda
- National University of Rwanda, Rwanda
- National University of Science and Technology, Zimbabwe (NUST)
- Open University of Tanzania, Dar-es-Salaam, Tanzania
- Togo University, Benin
- Uganda Martyrs University, Uganda
- Uganda Polytechnic, Uganda
- University of Abidjan, Ivory Coast
- University of Abou Moumouny of Niamey, Niger
- University of Benin, Benin
- University of Cape Coast, Ghana
- University of Cheikh Anta Diop, Senegal
- University of Dar-es-Salaam, Tanzania

- University of Eduardo Mondlane, Mozambique
- University of Ghana, Ghana
- University of Mozambique, Mozambique
- University of Namibia, Namibia
- University of Noukchott, Mauritania
- University of Ouagadougou, Bokina Faso
- University of Science and Technology, Ghana (UST)
- University of Zimbabwe, Zimbabwe

The Implementation of AVU at Kenyatta University

As a distance educator I was sponsored by Kenyatta University to attend a conference on Distance Education in Washington DC in October 1996. Etienne Baranshamaje, architect of the AVU model, presented a paper at the conference and, surprisingly, Kenya had been excluded from countries listed to participate in the project. I discussed with Mr Baranshamaje the possible involvement of Kenya – particularly Kenyatta University – in the project. After the conference, I briefed our Vice Chancellor on the possibility of Kenyatta's involvement, and he quickly contacted the World Bank, which readily incorporated Kenya, and Kenyatta University in the pilot phase.

The AVU inaugural workshop in Addis Ababa in February 1997 was attended by a contingent of five people from Kenyatta University. Soon after, the contract was signed between the Kenya Government, the World Bank and COMSAT – the supplier of satellite equipment. Preparations for installations and renovations were completed, and the Satellite Receive Terminal was installed in June 1997. For Kenyatta University, AVU has come at an opportune moment to revitalise and supplement existing academic courses. The main goals and objectives of AVU are as follows:

- To provide quality and relevant courses in science, engineering and computer science, and short-term courses in related fields.
- To increase enrolment of students in highly demanded science and technology fields.
- To provide university education to deserving students who may have missed admission due to limited opportunities.
- To provide high quality and relevant professional courses and seminars to top-level managers, journalists, and teachers in relevant areas.
- To offer a structure that can generate income and revitalise some of the financial hardships experienced at the university.
- Capacity building for professors, lecturers and students in computer skills.

The AVU Network

Content production

The AVU network configuration originates at the studio location on the premises of the content-producing institution, or in a nearby facility leased by the institution. Each content site includes all equipment necessary for the origination of both live and pre-recorded instructional programmes, and for the provision of these programmes to either a local or a remote INTELSAT-compatible uplink earth station. The studio also includes equipment necessary to provide certain levels and kinds of interactivity, such as audio talkback for live programmes, and to facilitate such other related functions as satellite files. The personnel on location consist of the professor or lecturer and, typically, a programme technician. The broadcast can be either live or videotaped.

Satellite transmission

The signal from the content site is transmitted via a local provider, currently the Indiana State University system, to an uplink facility in Washington DC. AVU is currently contracted with COMSAT to relay the signal from Washington DC to Africa by way of the INTELSAT satellite system. AVU currently enjoys unlimited usage with INTELSAT who, in the pilot phase, has donated the equivalent of US$2,000,000 of satellite capacity to the project. The Technical Officer of AVU manages the network system.

Local support

Each SSA (Sub-Saharan Africa) partner institution is provided with all the equipment necessary to receive digital satellite transmission and a full complement of AVU programmes and services. The current funding source (roughly equivalent to US$54,000 per university) is the World Bank. In the future, funding for local infrastructure will be provided by the AVU franchise centres. The outdoor equipment provided by AVU includes the receive-only satellite antenna and necessary electronic equipment, integration hardware, and cabling. The indoor classroom equipment is designed to be 'user-friendly' and to enable maximum flexibility in the use of AVU programmes and services.

The indoor equipment unit includes two or more digital video receiver–decoders; one or more television monitors; one or more video cassette recorders; two multimedia personal computer systems; a push-to-talk telephone; a printer; a facsimile machine; a monitor and control (M&C) unit; a custom-designed equipment cabinet, and other miscellaneous components to help ensure ease of operation and uninterrupted programme reception. A comprehensive data handling and communications system has been designed to receive, store and process incoming high-speed broadcast data channels, and to provide each receiving site with an outbound data/audio talk-back link.

Classroom

The typical AVU classroom has been between 30 and 40 students, sitting at their desks watching the videotaped or live broadcast on a television monitor. During live broadcasts, students have the opportunity for real-time two-way interactivity with the instructor and the ability to collaborate with other students.

The AVU Pilot Programmes in Kenyatta University

During the pilot phase, AVU had three semesters during which courses were transmitted from universities in Canada, Europe and America (Table 2.5, page 56).

All the students registered for these AVU courses were regular, on-campus students from departments of physics, mathematics, chemistry, and appropriate technology, which are part of the Faculty of Science. However, some of the core courses, including

Introduction to Engineering, Computer Architecture and Design, and Introduction to Internet are not offered in Kenyatta University.

Table 2.5 AVU Courses During the Pilot Phase

Course	Origination
Calculus I	New Jersey Institute of Technology (USA)
Calculus II	New Jersey Institute of Technology (USA)
Computer Organisation and Architecture	Colorado State University (USA)
Differential Equations	New Jersey Institute of Technology (USA)
Introduction to C++ Programming	Mount Saint Vincent University (Canada)
Introduction to Computing	University of Massachusetts (USA)
Introduction to Engineering	Georgia Institute of Technology (USA)
Introduction to Internet	University of Massachusetts (USA)
Organic Chemistry	Laurentian University (Canada)
Physics	Carleton University (Canada)

An Analysis of University Courses Offered through AVU Satellite

Table 2.6 Enrolment in University Units and Courses Offered through AVU's Satellite

Course	Number of students enrolled			
	Summer semester	Semester 1 1997	Semester 2 1998	Total
Calculus I	28	41	41	110
Calculus II	–	55	57	112
Computer Architecture and Organisation	–	–	41	41
Differential Equations	–	–	12	12
Introduction to C++ Programming	–	–	28	28
Introduction to Computing			20	20
Introduction to Engineering	–	–	20	20
Introduction to Internet		47	26	73
Organic Chemistry	–	–	31	31
Physics	–	24	23	47
Total	**28**	**167**	**299**	**494**

Enrolment has been increasing since the first courses were offered in the 1996–97 academic year. The trend in total number of students who did their units through the AVU's satellite facility is reflected in Table 2.6 (page 56) and Figure 2.1(page 58).

Gender disparity is evident, with males outnumbering females in almost all the units, as shown in Tables 2.7, 2.8 and 2.9 (page 59). Figures 2.2, 2.3 (pages 58 and 59) and 2.4 (page 61) represent this information graphically.

Table 2.7 Enrolment of Students in the First AVU Semester,
1 October –23 December 1997

Course	Number of students			
	Females	*Males*	*Total*	*Dropouts*
Calculus I	13	28	**41**	11
Calculus II	9	46	**55**	22
Introduction to Internet	6	41	**47**	6
Physics	0	24	**24**	3
Total	**28**	**139**	**167**	**42**

Table 2.8 Enrolment of Students in the Second AVU Semester,
26 January –15 May 1998

Course	Number of students			
	Females	*Males*	*Dropouts*	*Total*
Calculus I	10	20	11	**41**
Calculus II	7	26	24	**57**
Computer Architecture and Organisation	3	34	4	**41**
Differential Equations	3	9	–	**12**
Introduction to C++ Programming	2	26	7	**28**
Introduction to Computing	4	16	–	**20**
Introduction to Engineering	2	18	–	**20**
Introduction to Internet	5	21	–	**26**
Organic Chemistry	1	29	1	**31**
Physics	0	17	6	**23**
Total	**30**	**169**	**46**	**245**

Women's participation in AVU courses is no different from the national representation of girls in university, where less than 30 per cent are women. The picture is worse in facilities such as engineering and computer science. For instance, in Kenyatta University, women constitute 23 per cent in the Faculty of Science. This means that a relatively small number of women opt for AVU courses, as compared with men. This imbalance does not start at university, but at primary level. Studies indicate that Science and Mathematics are generally perceived to be 'masculine' subjects. The negative perception about girls' ability to study sciences, and other factors related to cultural attitudes, poverty and poor performance, contribute to the low level of participation of girls in science subjects at tertiary level.

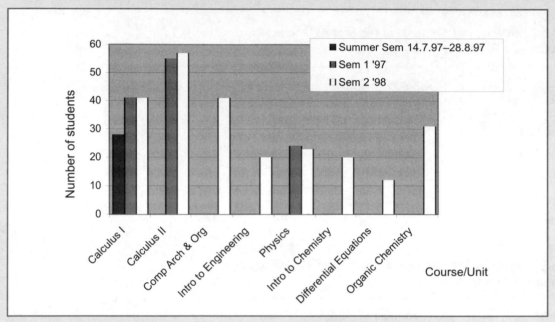

Figure 2.1 Enrolment in University Units and Courses Offered through AVU's Satellite, 1997–98

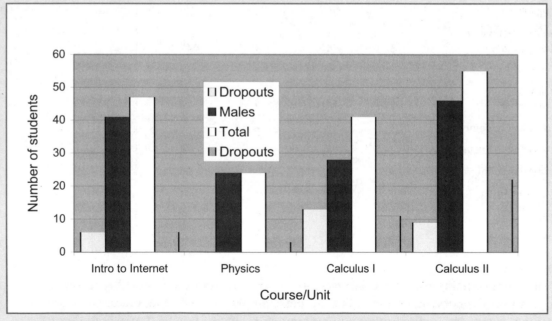

Figure 2.2 Enrolment in University Units and Courses Offered through AVU's Satellite, 1997–98, by Gender

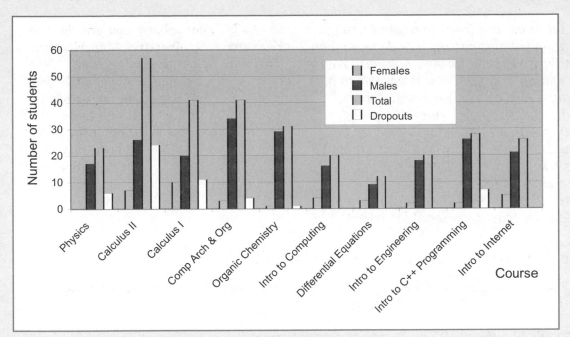

*Figure 2.3 Enrolment in AVU Units and Courses, Second Semester,
26 January–15 May 1998, by Gender*

Calculus I

Twenty-eight students from the Department of Mathematics at Kenyatta University registered for the AVU Summer Semester opted for an AVU course in Mathematics, Calculus I, originating from New Jersey Institute of Technology (NJIT), USA, and delivered by Professor Rose Dios (Table 2.9). Students' comments about the course, reproduced here and on page 60, show how much they enjoyed these lectures.

*Table 2.9 Enrolment in AVU's 'Calculus I'
Course, Summer Semester, 1997*

Course	Number of students		
	Females	*Males*	*Total*
Calculus I	6	22	28

The other Mathematics students continued with their traditional Kenyatta University lecturer during the summer semester. Two continuous assessment tests and one final examination were given at the end of the semester. The local AVU instructor from the Mathematics Department set and marked the examination, which experienced a pass rate of 80 per cent compared with a mere 40 per cent in the traditional mode of delivery (which, as pointed out by the teacher who taught both courses, consists of lectures and a few demonstrations).

It is important to mention that for all courses except for Internet and Introduction to Computing, interested students from related departments at the University register for AVU courses. Before AVU was adopted at Kenyatta University, the Senate approved the integration

*'Professor Dios is a very good teacher because her lectures start with simple examples and build slowly to complex examples (i.e.) from 'known to unknown'. This approach enables me to understand and enjoy Mathematics.'
(Personal interview, first Calculus I student)*

'It has taken me two times to retake Calculus I examination without passing. I had given up on Calculus I if it were not for AVU Calculus I course which I managed to pass. It was possible to pass because AVU courses provide textbooks, comprehensive notes, tutorial sessions, interaction with an instructor in America and a local university lecturer who always explains concepts during tutorials. During revision, we get pre-recorded videotapes to review lectures. Therefore, all these benefits enabled me to pass.'
(Female student, personal interview)

of AVU pilot phase courses in the Kenyatta University curriculum. Therefore semester grades from AVU courses were computed along with other grades in the respective departments. Two groups of students, one taking the traditional course and the other the AVU course, provide an opportunity for comparison in terms of participation and performance.

The First AVU Semester (1 October – 23 December 1997)

The full semester of the pilot phase started in October. The registration of students is shown in Table 2.7 (page 57 above).

'Before I joined AVU courses, I had never seen a computer nor sat before a keyboard, but from the Internet course, I have known how to use the computer, send e-mail, design websites and access courses, data etc. from the websites.' (Personal interview, AVU student)

Introduction to Internet

This course generated a great deal of enthusiasm from students, faculty members and the general public (as is demonstrated by the comments on this page). It was over-subscribed, with more than 400 students registering, but due to limited facilities only 40 students were admitted to the course. A loan of Ksh 5 million (US$86,000) from the University was given to AVU to purchase 20 computers and one projector for internet training, and a separate laboratory was created for training. AVU–Kenyatta instituted income-generating measures to offset the loan and meet some of the running costs of AVU. Students paid Ksh 15,000 (US$280) per semester for the Internet course.

Of the first Internet class, 22 students have been employed by companies in Nairobi.

Performance in AVU Courses

'I am only a third year Physics student, from very poor family background, struggling to complete fourth year fees for January 1998. Fortunately, after my Internet examination in December 1997, I managed to apply for a job with Commercial Bank of Africa, Nairobi, attended an interview, performed very well in both theory and practicals, and was employed even before completing my degree course in Physics and Mathematics. The AVU Internet course has earned me a job!!' (Interview, AVU student, December 1997)

Performance in AVU courses and units has been good, except for Calculus I and Computer Architecture and Organisation, whose average scores were below 50 per cent during the Summer semester and the Second semester in 1998. Performance has been particularly good in computer-related courses, with average scores of over 70 per cent for the last two semesters (Table 2.10 and Figure 2.4).

Table 2.10 AVU Course Performance, by Semester

Course	Average marks		
	Summer sem. 1997	*Semester 1 1998*	*Semester 2 1998*
Calculus I	46	51	–
Calculus II	–	–	51
Computer Architecture and Organisation	–	–	46
Differential Equations	–	–	63
Introduction to C++ Programming	–	–	76
Introduction to Computing	–	–	78
Introduction to Engineering	–	–	61
Introduction to Internet	–	77	74
Organic Chemistry	–	–	62
Physics	–	56	–

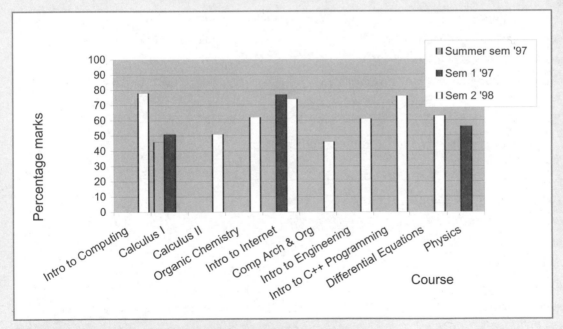

Figure 2.4 AVU Course Performance, by Semester

Apart from AVU semester programmes, which targeted campus students, there are short computer courses (Table 2.11, page 62) lasting from two weeks to one or two months, depending on the nature of the course. These courses run from 0800 hours to 2200 hours and are open to the public for professional upgrading and continuous learning. The target groups include civil servants, people working for organisations such as banks, ministries, parastatals and universities, graduates, doctors and school leavers. Enrolment figures for these courses are shown in Tables 2.12 and 2.13.

Table 2.11 AVU Short Computer Courses

Code	Title
AVU 01	Introduction to Microcomputers and MS-DOS
AVU 02	Windows '95
AVU 03	MS Word '97
AVU 04	MS Access '97
AVU 05	MS Excel '97
AVU 21	Using Internet
AVU 22	Advanced Internet
AVU 31	C++ Programming
AVU 34	Visual Basic Programming

Table 2.12 Enrolment in AVU Short Computer Courses, by Phase

	Duration	Females	Males	Total
Phase 1	29 May 1998 to 24 July 1998	87	189	**276**
Phase 2	27 July 1998 to 2 October 1998	125	337	**462**
Phase 3	12 October 1998 to 18 December 1998	106	125	**251**

Table 2.13 Enrolment in AVU Short Computer Courses per Phase, by Course

	Phase 1	Phase 2	Phase 3	Total
AVU 01	57	116	105	**278**
AVU 02	62	97	92	**251**
AVU 03	45	67	–	**112**
AVU 04	41	66	–	**107**
AVU 05	40	65	–	**105**
AVU 21	13	23	21	**57**
AVU 22	10	20	14	**44**
AVU 31	8	8	–	**16**
AVU 34	–	–	19	**19**
Total	**276**	**462**	**251**	**989**

Statistics and the summary graphs show that enrolment in the AVU short computer courses has been very good. The most popular course, Introduction to Microcomputers and Ms-Dos, enrolled more than 100 students in the last two phases. Enrolment has been higher for males than for females, but this discrepancy is decreasing with time, as reflected in Figures 2.5, 2.6 and 2.7 (page 64).

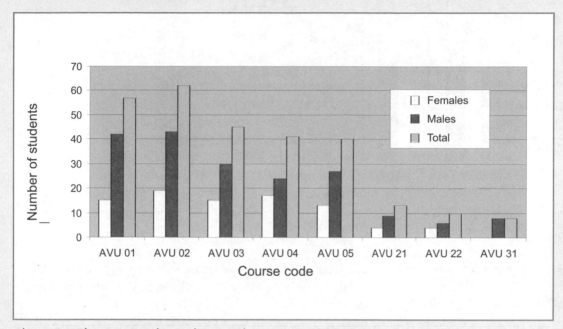

Figure 2.5 Phase 1: Enrolment in AVU Short Computer Courses

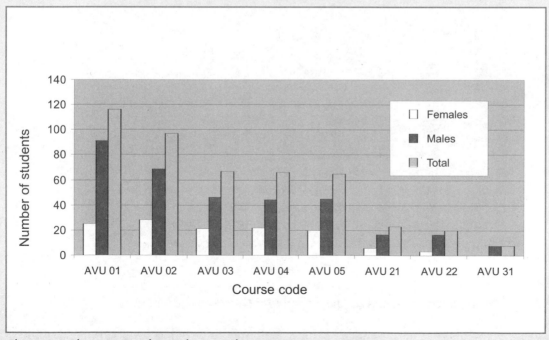

Figure 2.6 Phase 2: Enrolment in AVU Short Computer Courses

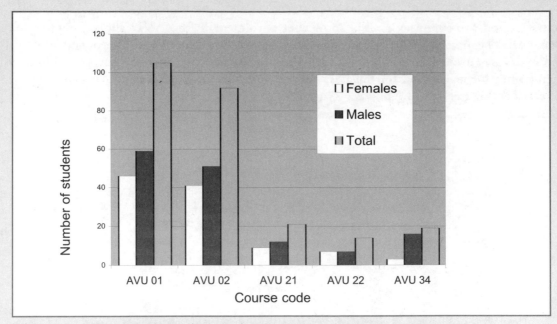

Figure 2.7 Phase 3: Enrolment in AVU Short Computer Courses

Phase 2 recorded the highest number of students in most of the courses, but a valid conclusion about the enrolment trend can only be made after Phase 3. We can only note that there is a slight decline in enrolment, as reflected in Figure 2.8.

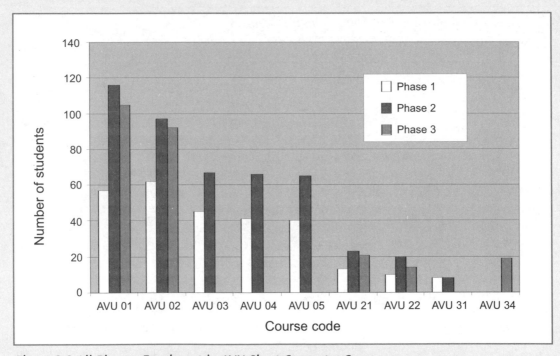

Figure 2.8 All Phases: Enrolment in AVU Short Computer Courses

Figure 2.9 reveals that performance in these computer courses has been very good, with mean scores of over 70 per cent in all courses.

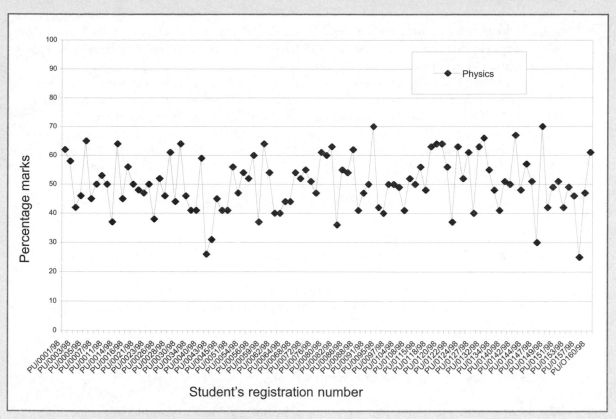

Figure 2.16 AVU Pre-University Physics Results

Table 2.15 AVU Pre-University Programme: Distribution of Scores by Course

Course		Calculus I (Math III)	Chemistry 100	Introduction to Computer Science	Physics 105	
Range	Grade					Average
Above 70%	A	11	11	7	2	3
60–69%	B	17	28	13	20	15
50–59%	C	30	23	22	32	36
40–49%	D	21	25	31	38	37
Below 40%	E	19	12	23	9	10
	Total	**98**	**99**	**96**	**101**	**101**
Incomplete cases		3	2	5	–	–

The Management of AVU

With outsourcing the preferred mode of operation during the beta phase, the management staff of AVU consists of a small nucleus of full-time employees and a number of short-term, specialist consultants. Accounting and other office support are currently provided by the World Bank. Most of the organisational functions are outsourced in order to keep the organisation lean and focused, and the overhead costs low. Currently AVU management includes: Founder and Chief Executive Officer, Academic Director and Technical Director.

At each participating university, a campus co-ordinator assumes overall responsibility for local implementation of the AVU network. The co-ordinator provides leadership and guidance to faculty and staff members officially assigned to the positions of Course Moderator, Course Facilitator, and Technical Co-ordinator, and to others who assist in day-to-day implementation of the AVU network. Each course is moderated by a local instructor (expert in the discipline) who has the following responsibilities:

- serving as the primary liaison with AVU academic staff;
- grading homework and examinations;
- tutoring and advising students;
- serving as a faculty member to record and assign grades for students registered on the course;
- reviewing and reporting student academic and/discipline problems;
- providing guidance and counselling to students, and support to the course facilitator;
- reviewing the forms, logs and surveys forwarded by the course facilitator, and sending them to the campus co-ordinator for return to AVU; and
- attending training sessions provided by AVU.

The local course moderator is assisted by a junior graduate assistant course facilitator whose responsibilities are:

- facilitating instruction by following schedules, homework, examinations and laboratory work;
- retrieving course materials sent electronically or by other means, and making the required number for class registrants;
- turning and checking the equipment prior to the class;
- recording attendance at each class.

The facilitator assists the course moderator in tutoring and advising students.

AVU Seminars

After adequate marketing of AVU seminars among the business community in Nairobi, 40 executive managers from companies such as Barclays Bank, Standard Chartered Bank, Central Bank, Kenya Commercial Bank, Commercial Bank of Africa and Kenya Breweries attended a seminar on 'Purchasing Policies and Practices' transmitted 'live' from Virginia Technology, USA, on 14 and 21 August 1997. There was an overwhelming response from the business community. During the live seminar, participants interacted with Professor Murphy from Virginia Technology and their counterparts from Uganda, Zimbabwe and Ethiopia. The virtual seminar was extremely exciting, and drew favourable comments from participants, some of which are reproduced here.

'It is unbelievable that a virtual typical of situations in America is taking a place in Kenya. This is the first time in my life to participate in a seminar of this nature.'

Commenting on the technology, one participant emphasised that, 'The use of modern technology enhanced proper learning and sustained our span of concentration.'

This was a very successful seminar which indicated collaboration between the business community and the University. Such support augurs well for sustainability of the project, since participants will be expected to pay for such courses in future.

In addition to the Virginia Technology Seminar, a series of training seminars was organised by the Economic Development Institute (EDI) of the World Bank. Starting on 31 March 1998 , 30 journalists from Kenya attended 14 weekly seminars (from 1900 hours to 2200 hours), delivered by live satellite transmission at Kenyatta University AVU.

The EDI seminars were an income-generating venture – EDI paid AVU-Kenyatta University a total of US$5,000 for using the AVU infrastructure to transmit courses to journalists. Several other important seminars have been held at AVU-Kenyatta, including YK2000 seminars; Balanced Score Card, and Strategy and Innovation.

'The case study approach gave solutions to practical problems in an organisation.'

'The seminar was very educative, informative, and enriched what I already knew on purchasing.'

'I feel like I am in Washington D.C. attending EDI seminar, we can ask questions easily and interact clearly with course instructions as if the delivery was face to face. It is so 'real' that I cannot believe we are in Kenya'.
(Participant at first AVU transmission)

The Impact of AVU on Kenyatta University

For the seventeen months (from June 1997) that AVU has existed in Kenya, it has had considerable impact on students, faculty members and the entire community. The following achievements have been experienced:

· *Provision of educational resources.* One hundred and twenty computers for the AVU enable students to participate effectively in computer courses – Internet Access, Introduction to Computing, Computer Programming C++, Computer Architecture and Organisation. Before the emergence of AVU, the University had extremely limited resources of computers – the Computer Centre had only four computers, and the Mathematics Department three –which were inadequate for courses. Students who enroll for AVU courses are provided with textbooks and notes. The trickle effects of AVU resources have permeated the entire University Science students' community. Internet facilities provided by AVU are utilised by everyone interested in accessing e-mail and internet search. Thus, e-mail facility has modernised the university environment.

· *Introduction of new courses.* Computer science as a discipline has never existed in Kenyatta University, but with the emergence of AVU, many computer-based courses have become very popular. The Internet course, for instance, is very new and students find it lucrative since it opens up job-prospects. As a result of these new information technologies the University, assisted by AVU students, has created a website.

· *Capacity building.* A culture of continuing education has been perpetuated through AVU computer-related courses, among professors, lecturers, students and the public. Seminars and workshops have attracted the executive cadre of the business community who find relevant courses via satellite very 'educative and refreshing', especially teleconferencing – interactive technology which empowers them to communicate with their counterparts in Africa and Europe. Enhancement of local capacities to participate in activities within the country and in Africa offers an opportunity for sharing expertise within the region. For instance, qualified engineers – the technical co-ordinator of AVU and the campus co-ordinator – effectively assist in setting up satellite technology in other African countries. This means that Kenyatta University experts assist other countries and enhance sustainability and maintenance of AVU within Africa.

With regard to courses, AVU will make a significant impact by providing training opportunities to secondary school leavers. Currently, of the estimated 150,000 students who complete secondary school annually, about 7–8 per cent are admitted to universities, and a further 15–20 per cent to other tertiary institutions, leaving over 30 per cent of qualified students without places.

· *Income-generating and increase in enrolment.* Through AVU, Kenyatta University will increase its enrolment with students who will pay for AVU degree courses. Currently, interested members of the public pay for short AVU courses in computer-related fields – for example the EDI seminar for journalists generated income for the University. Income generated through AVU courses in 1998 is reflected in Figure 2.17. Figure 2.18 shows total AVU expenditure for that period.

· *Digital library.* AVU maintains a sophisticated internet-based digital library of journals, academic studies and textbooks that allows students and staff to access the world database of information. This web-based resource provides a one-stop-shop for current research materials unavailable in local libraries. Users of the AVU digital library can log on to the database by providing a user name and password in order to connect to various articles, journals and abstracts. The AVU digital library enables accessibility to over 1,700 current journals and texts. However, no part of such material shall be published, stored in a retrieval system or transmitted in any form or by any means, without permission from copyright

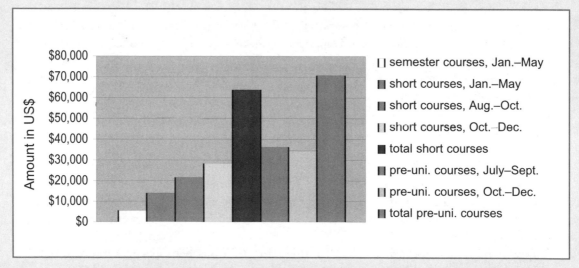

Figure 2.17 Income Generated through AVU-Kenyatta Courses, January–December 1998

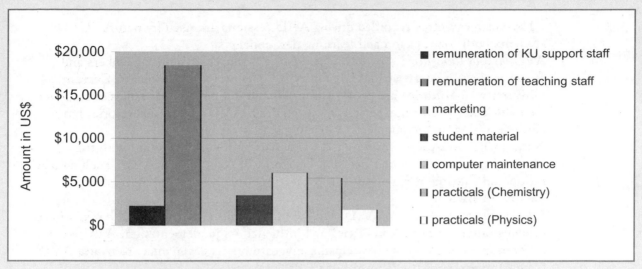

Figure 2.18 AVU-Kenyatta Total Expenditure, January–December 1998

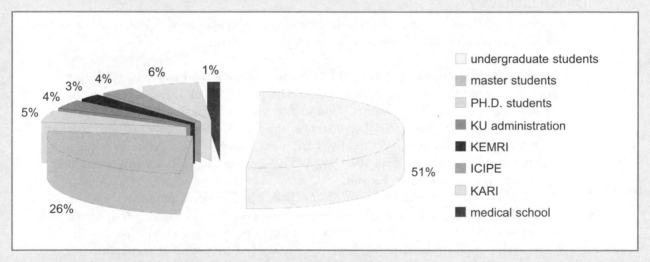

Figure 2.19 The Use of AVU Digital Library, July–December 1998

owners. Library users have access to the database and the opportunity to copy documents within the copyright regulations. Library search is done for those unable to use the internet access facility, at a small fee. At the time of writing, the digital library has been in use for six months. Figure 2.19 shows the proportions of students, lecturers and researchers who have used it.

· *Challenge to University faculty members.* The AVU mode of delivery has challenged some lecturers and unconsciously improved their teaching strategies. The observations of one physics course moderator are reproduced here.

'I used to think that I was one of the best Physics lecturers in the world. But listening to professors from America, and their teaching approaches, I have had to evaluate myself and rate my competence! In essence, I have borrowed some of their case study approaches in teaching, which seems to appeal to my students.'

The video cassettes recorded during AVU sessions are used by non-AVU students both for revision and learning new concepts.

· *AVU virtual laboratories supplement existing resources.* Faculty members and students share modern virtual laboratory equipment and experiments. Current University laboratories are poorly equipped, and due to lack of resources students have difficulty perform experiments as required. AVU virtual laboratories have come as a 'saviour' to supplement existing scanty resources.

· *Networking.* Kenyatta University AVU assists and works together with the Universities of Nairobi and Egerton. Egerton will soon launch AVU. Such collaboration and sharing of resources is a cornerstone for the success of the AVU 'family' in Africa.

· *Participatory Advocacy of AVU.* Unlike other projects of the World Bank, where officials initiate a project in Africa and influence its implementation, AVU has a different approach, where participants advocate for its acceptance. Kenyatta AVU is 'our project', not the 'World Bank's Project'.

The Challenges

There are pertinent challenges which impinge on operations of AVU in Africa. The following challenges are significant, particularly to Kenya:

· *Electricity interruptions.* Power fluctuations in Africa tend to affect satellite receive terminal, particularly computers. The power 'black outs' or 'change of power' in the case of generators, tend to damage hard disks and sometimes the system boards of computers. For instance, the DELL computers (Seagate) used at AVU-Kenyatta have a lower quality hard disk, which is susceptible in times of irregular power supply, than the QUANTUM, whose hard disk is more resilient and can recover after a black out.

· *Lack of a clear national communications policy in Kenya.* Communication services are strategic infrastructure; therefore private ownership of Kenya's telecommunications services is limited. Privatisation and liberalisation go hand-in-hand with ownership, and multinationals have not been given that kind of ownership in Kenya. Telecommunications services are very expensive, for two main reasons: first, Kenya Posts and Telecommunications (KPTC) has a monopoly on services; second, Kenya does not yet own an internet 'hub', and so local internet service providers have hubs in the USA, Canada and Europe. The cost of international links is very high, resulting in expensive internet services for local consumers. AVU relies heavily on the internet and e-mail.

· *Slow internet connectivity at AVU-Kenyatta.* Internet access is very slow, due to the mode of connection which is 'dial-up' using a telephone line. The following reasons contribute to slow access:

  – The band width for signal over the telephone lines in Kenya is normally very slow, with the highest rate of transfer averaging 19.2 kbps (kilo bits per second).

  – The telephone line signal is of very poor quality, resulting in average signal loss and errors. AVU therefore suffers from connection cuts and loss of link which make sending and receiving mail frustrating.

– Heavy access of the internet by users in the Western world creates 'traffic jams'. This happens during the day, interrupting internet courses at the AVU.
– Frequent 'link' breakdowns due to natural or physical calamities (such as flooding of cables), including breakdown at the KPTC Satellite Earth Station which may last one day, cutting off all forms of telecommunication between the whole country and the outside world; frequent maintenance of KPTC telecommunications equipment, resulting sometimes in loss of communication for a day or two; telephone problems due to breakdown at the University exchange, blocking out phone calls for hours, and occasional cases of the Internet Service Provider (ISP) pilot telephone line going out of order and causing frustration and anxiety as dialling and connection become very difficult.

These challenges do not in any way undermine the effectiveness and impact of AVU in Kenya. Rather they have influenced AVU Kenyatta to try to overcome the obstacles. At the national level, a bill on Kenya's posts and telecommunications policy is soon to be tabled in Parliament. It is hoped that with a policy framework, postal and communications services will be liberalised and better services ensured.

KPTC is expected to launch a national hub or 'backbone' by end of December 1998. This should facilitate fast and affordable internet access by higher learning institutions.

The Way Forward for the AVU Project at Kenyatta University

The on-going pilot phase generated much enthusiasm and viable prospects for the operational phase, which will start in October 1999. The following measures are being put in place to accommodate the onset of full degree courses during the operational phase:

· *AVU curriculum development*. African scholars with expertise in computer science, engineering, physics, chemistry, mathematics and computer engineering were selected to participate in an AVU curriculum development and design workshop in Washington DC in May 1998. Courses have been developed by both African scholars and their counterparts in America, Europe and Canada.
· *Management and Sustainability of AVU*. For the operational phase and future sustainability of the project, AVU is to be managed in a business-like manner. Each site will form a business company with limited liabilities. Kenyatta AVU is in the process of forming a company in which the University will have shares. The company will be responsible for generating income and meeting its loan and recurrent costs. The following income-generating courses and activities will be offered at AVU Kenyatta:
  – *Degree courses*: Computer Science, Computer Engineering, and a MBA course;
  – *Diploma courses*: Introduction to Computing and Computer Programming C++;
  – *Certificate short courses*: top-executive seminars in business management; school teachers' seminars in computer education; virtual seminars for journalists; virtual seminars for army officers, etc.;
  – *In-service courses*: professional development courses for professors, lecturers, etc. in computer science, and for secondary- and primary-school teachers;
  – *Digital AVU libraries*: minimal fee charge for faculty members to access information, and (as part of their AVU fees) for students.

- *Cyber café*: open to students and faculty members at a fee;
- *Business facility centre*;
- *Photocopying*: e-mail and fax;
- *Internet Service provider (ISP)*: Kenyatta will soon access a server, and modalities for the service are being put in place. Companies around Nairobi will subscribe to the AVU internet provider;
- *Consultancy section*: consultancy proposals will be presented to business companies for funding, and projects will be undertaken by the AVU to generate income.

Summary and Conclusions

The rapid expansion of university education and increased enrolment in Kenya and elsewhere in sub-Saharan Africa have not been accompanied by a commensurate rise in the level of government funding, to ensure a high quality of instruction. In many universities there are therefore serious problems related to instructional quality, class sizes and availability of facilities and materials. The AVU, supported by the World Bank, has been initiated to offer new technologies to overcome such barriers. Through the use of digital-satellite technology, programmes in some science subjects are being transmitted from several universities in the North, and these have been well received by both students and staff at Kenyatta University, which is one of the participating universities. The programmes have a high potential for expansion, capacity building, income generation, and networking among universities in sub-Saharan Africa.

Although the AVU programme appears to be a promising innovation, pertinent issues relating to sustainability require serious consideration. Among them is that of cost. The programme is heavily capital intensive, particularly in the purchase and maintenance of the satellite receive terminal equipment which host universities will have to shoulder after World Bank assistance is phased out.

With proper management, accountability, strategic planning and marketing of AVU programmes, there is great hope and promise for AVU in revitalising university systems in Kenyatta and inculcating the notion of income-generation and self-reliance in university management.

References

AVU (1997), *The Campus Co-ordinator Manual for 1997* Prototype Phase.

AVU (1997), *The Course Co-ordinator Manual for the Prototype Phase.*

AVU (1997), *Inaugural Training Workshop Manual: Addis-Ababa 16-21 February.*

Baranshamaje, E., *The African Virtual University*, concept paper, Washington DC.

Harris, H. (1996), *The African Virtual University Library*, Washington DC.

Juma, M.N. (1997), *AVU Progress Reports*, Kenyatta University.

Republic of Kenya (1997), *Economic Survey 1997*, Nairobi, Government Printer.

Sifuna, D. N. (1997), *The Governance of Kenyan Public Universities*, Education Research Series no. 1, Nairobi, Lyceum Educational Consultants.

World Bank (1998), *Education in Sub-Saharan Africa, Policies for Adjustment, Revitalization and Expansion*, Washington DC, World Bank.

3 Technology for Management and Efficiency in Education

Understanding the Issues

Centralised and Decentralised Education Systems

Successful management of education systems has always depended on having the necessary information available, as much as on having personnel trained and experienced in management. It is equally important to have this information in a timely manner, and in a form appropriate for the intended purpose. Information enables education officials to keep their fingers on the pulse of the system, and make sensible decisions affecting the status and routine administration of education in the country. This entails having a wide range of information about learners, teachers, facilities and resources that make up an education system. For each of these categories different kinds of information are required, depending on the purpose, and on the level of decision-making at which the information is to be used. In this regard it is important to distinguish between centralised and decentralised education systems, since this factor helps to determine the level at which various kinds of information are used for making decisions or for taking action related to the system.

In highly centralised systems it is often the case that teachers, who collect the data at source, do not have a stake in the use of much of the information they are expected to collect. Generally data is collected as a matter of routine and out of a sense of duty, rather than for intrinsic professional reasons. In decentralised systems, however, where many decisions are taken locally, teachers and school heads tend to be more aware of the strong links between information collected and the management or decision-making process they are expected to perform. There is therefore a strong case for decentralisation in education, since it is likely that data will be collected more meticulously and used more appropriately in a decentralised education system than in a highly centralised one.

In large Commonwealth countries such as Australia, Britain, Canada, India, Nigeria and Pakistan the education system has traditionally been decentralised. This is usually due to the existence of a fairly decentralised form of government in which there are strong local authorities in charge of education. In the small states of the Commonwealth, their size suggests that they will continue to have a more centralised system of government. But even in small states, devolution of authority and decision-making powers to schools is a growing trend in education.

In most other Commonwealth countries, however, the system of government has been recently in a state of transition, from highly centralised to fairly decentralised. International and pan-Commonwealth efforts to strengthen democracy through greater transparency and accountability have given rise to a new trend that emphasises greater decentralisation of government. In addition to this wider socio-political pressure, there have been pressures from within education systems for greater decentralisation. This stems from growing criticism of education systems that offer a centrally designed curriculum that is not relevant to some communities. Increased budgetary difficulties have also meant that local communities are being required to play an increasing role in the financing of education. With these and similar critical trends in education, many countries have made intensive efforts to decentralise their education systems. The main concern has been to make education more relevant to local needs and more accountable to the local communities that schools are supposed to serve.

Reasonable success has been achieved in this area, but the Education Management Information System (EMIS) in many of these countries still suffers from a range of difficulties, including the negative effects of a 'centralised culture'. This means, for instance, that in some countries the Ministry of Education still does not have adequate or reliable disaggregated statistics on the education system. The problem is often due to poor record-keeping and inefficient data collection as the system goes through the transition from a centralised to a more decentralised structure. At each level, from the schools to the district offices, to the provincial offices, up to the central ministry, there are weaknesses in the generation, storage, retrieval and use of information for management purposes. However, even in countries that have a fairly efficient EMIS in place, there can be difficulties and weaknesses in this area.

Problems with EMIS

Weaknesses in EMIS generally stem first from a lack of motivation for proper collection and handling of management information. Data collection and record-keeping tasks can easily be seen as imposing an extra administrative burden on teachers and school heads, unless they themselves appreciate and make use of such information for intrinsic professional reasons. In Britain, for instance, recent Labour government policy on the quality of education and moves towards verifiable national standards, have prompted reactions protesting against an envisaged rise in the workload of teachers due to an increase in required testing and record-keeping. Clearly, even in a decentralised education system with a good EMIS tradition, national policies and strategies can have a controversial impact on the amount of work involved in the collection and management of information at local as well as national levels.

The question of motivation therefore becomes important for those who are expected to take on such an additional workload. What is most critical in this respect is the kind of professional motivation that can be achieved when teachers and school heads readily identify with the new policies and strategies, and are keen to implement them fully. Motivation alone is not always adequate, for any new or additional workload has implications for the efficiency with which normal duties like teaching and administration are carried out in schools. Besides there are also controversial issues concerning fair remuneration and adequate benefits for additional work.

The second source of problems and weaknesses in EMIS stems from accountability or the lack of it. This is particularly true of highly centralised education systems that require information to be collected routinely and passed upwards through a hierarchy of bureaucratic levels. This kind of centralised culture often means that there is a relative lack of accountability at the local level, so that sloppy collection, inefficient handling or outright false manipulation of information has no clear or immediate repercussions. In the worst cases enrolment figures can be inflated and staff numbers increased artificially, where an institution stands to benefit from this in terms of resource allocation or supplement for teachers' salaries. Many developing Commonwealth countries have suffered a drain on their scarce education resources, due to the phenomenon of 'ghost teachers' and 'phantom pupils'. Similarly there have been problems with malpractice in the conduct of national examinations at the local level and in the compilation of performance data for use at the national level.

A third major reason for weaknesses in EMIS is lack of training. It is necessary to provide proper training for teachers and school heads if they are expected to perform data collection tasks in an efficient and reliable manner. This is not simply a matter of training them to make entries in the various record documents. It involves developing the skills to carry out initial processing of data so that it can be presented in a form that is useful at the school level and beyond. Teachers and school heads need to understand and appreciate some of the uses to which such information can be put for various purposes and at various stages in the system. Moreover, training should provide them with an appreciation of the importance of errors and the techniques for minimising them in data collection and processing. Providing appropriate training in these areas is likely to remain a major problem for many developing Commonwealth countries whose education systems have a high proportion of teachers without even the basic pedagogical and professional training. However, there have been some successful attempts, which demonstrate that training for data collection and processing can be provided readily through a series of in-service programmes.

A fourth and critical factor that accounts for weaknesses in EMIS is the means of doing things – the predominant EMIS technology. The means of collecting and processing information determines the quality of the EMIS from the collection of raw data, through various stages of collation and analysis, to the point at which it is used for action and decision-making. In situations where information is generated and stored using the most basic means, such as written entries in attendance registers, mark books, record cards and report forms, the process is very laborious for both teachers and school heads. There is increased chance of error at the information-collection stage, and in subsequent processing of the information at the local level. With such basic means of recording and storing data and information, it is very difficult to use it fully and efficiently. For instance, it is necessary to trawl through the various record documents in order to compile any kind of aggregate information required for action and decision-making. It is also difficult to transfer such data to other points in the system where it may be needed for making decisions or taking action.

Where low-technology EMIS is prevalent, transfer of data and information is a serious problem. Frequently information has to be transported physically from schools to district offices where it is collated and processed. The results then have to be taken physically to provincial offices, where the same process takes place, and again the processed information needs to be taken physically to the central ministry. This manual transfer of data and information invariably involves the use of school heads and inspectors (with associated transport costs) in order to guarantee 'safe delivery'. Moreover, in some countries this has come to be seen as one of the most important functions of school heads and inspectors, with the data usually being treated as prized confidential material. In practice this means that expensive supervisory and managerial staff are being used essentially as postal agents in the education system.

Another major problem resulting from the manual collection, processing and transfer of information is that of time lag. The typical time-lag chain starts with delays at the school level in collecting and processing the required data. This means that districts do not have the information they need in time to make important decisions. They cannot provide the provincial offices with the necessary information on time, and in turn the central ministry cannot get the information it requires in a timely manner. All of this means that decisions on the allocation of resources, posting of teachers, supply of materials and so on, often have to be made on old information or on guesswork. It also means that users of the system – including students, parents, local communities, government departments and employers – cannot readily access important educational information in a timely and reliable manner.

The issue of transfer of data and information is important also because it influences attitudes towards its collection, processing and storage. In principle there is a tension between local and central use of such information. The question that then arises is whether data is collected and processed mainly for use at the school level or simply for transmission to levels beyond the school. It needs to be appreciated that there is usually a trade-off between the collection and processing of management information on the one hand, and getting on with the professional tasks of teaching and learning on the other hand. Understandably, excessive demand to collect and process data can be regarded by teachers and school heads as an unwelcome burden if much of this is simply for transfer to levels beyond the school. However, if such information is seen as beneficial to the work of the school and its accountability to the community it serves, there is likely to be a much greater degree of willingness and even enthusiasm to carry out the tasks involved in data collection and processing.

Quite apart from educational data, it is often necessary to make use of additional data from outside the education system to promote proper planning and management. This usually includes data on population characteristics, household incomes, community profiles and labour market trends. Typically, most of this kind of data is not captured in the conventional EMIS that tends to be more focused on standard educational data. There is therefore a wide range of educational and external information required for proper planning and management of education systems.

The Rationale for Collecting and Processing Data

Against this background of information needs and weaknesses in the collection and processing of data, it is important to appreciate that these activities are not simply ends in themselves, but are the means to something else. The rationale for collecting and processing data is to facilitate informed decision-making and sensible action in the best interest of education. Efforts to improve data collection and processing are not to be pursued at the expense of these wider objectives. In this regard there are at least three levels of problems faced by many developing Commonwealth countries.

First is the issue of what is worth collecting and the quality of what is being collected. In some cases, even where there are commendable efforts to keep proper records, the quality of the data collected is so suspect that its usefulness is doubtful. Many developing countries have made commendable progress in this area, in so far as they can at least provide reliable aggregate figures for such basics as enrolment, staff numbers and even educational expenditures. However, most of these countries still have much work to do when it comes to improving the quality and reliability of more disaggregated data or other critical categories of data. This is often because data is typically aggregated at various levels (district, province, etc.) before it reaches the central ministry. Many countries have made progress with the collection of school-level data that can facilitate disaggregated indicators at the central ministry level. Success in this area depends not only on improved processing capacity, but on reliable record-keeping at the school level. Efficient transmission of data to the central ministry and other levels where it is needed for various purposes is also important. In each of these areas it is necessary to explore fully the possible ways in which technology can best be used to enhance performance.

Second is the question of what is done with the data collected. For most countries where collection of raw data is a problem, useful analysis of that data presents an even bigger problem. This has a lot to do with the transition from simply collecting and tabulating data to interpreting and analysing it. There are standard statistical techniques for processing data of course, but decisions as to what indicators should be extracted from it, and why, are at the heart of good analysis. These decisions in turn should help to determine what kind of data is worth collecting in the first instance. While many countries now routinely produce reliable standard statistics on enrolment, it is rare to have the same kind of indicators when it comes to such critical factors as lateness, absenteeism, drop-out and even repetition. Yet these are now regarded as being at the heart of understanding the complexities of access, retention and even achievement in education. They are also the main kinds of indicators that are most useful for local action and decision-making. The implication is that more and different kinds of data may have to be collected and analysed. Here again the use of technology needs to be fully explored as a means of facilitating improvements in the quality of data collection and analysis.

The third level of difficulty has to do with the quality of decision-making and action that results from the use of data processing and analysis as part of an EMIS. In far too many countries, the links between such analysis and policy decisions tend to be poor and tenuous at best. Yet the main reason for collecting and analysing data is to inform policy decisions and strategic action relating to the education system. The issue is more to do with interpretation and judgement than the use of technology *per se*. Increasingly, however, the use of sophisticated modelling techniques has been shown to be of great benefit in promoting improvements in decision-making based on data collected and analysed as part of an EMIS. On the one hand, good analysis means that information from the EMIS can provide a basis for proposing various alternative lines of action and policy decisions. On the other hand, good modelling based on the same information enables officials to project into the future and to discern the possible consequences of alternative policies, strategies and lines of action proposed for the education system.

This brief review of key issues has highlighted the fact that information is vital for management and efficiency in education. It has indicated that there are many complex issues to be considered in dealing with information that is likely to be useful to those who manage and take key decisions relating to education systems. These issues relate to the manner in which data is generated, stored, transmitted, retrieved, processed and used for planning and management at different levels of the education system. Clearly technology can play a pivotal role in enhancing an effective and efficient educational management information system. However, it is equally clear that technology is not a panacea for all the complex problems in this area. It is a tool that can contribute to solving these problems, rather than a solution in itself.

We need to assess carefully and systematically where, when and how to use different kinds of technology to develop an efficient and effective EMIS. This entails not just an understanding of what different technologies can do for us, but also some insight into why information is essential, what information is required for different purposes, and how such information is used in planning and management. It is only against such a background of understanding and insight that we can begin to put the role of technology in context and move towards making sensible choices related to the use of technology for management and efficiency in education.

Why Information is of the Essence

Information is the oxygen of good management. It determines the knowledge-base from which critical decisions are made and provides current as well as projected scenarios of the system for which decisions are being made. It indicates how far the goals and objectives set are being achieved; how efficiently the resources provided are being utilised, and how far the governing rules and regulations are being followed.

Information is essential to the life and well-being of education systems for at least three major reasons. First, it is important for proper management and decision-making in the routine administration of the system. In other words, an education system exists only in so far as there are recognisable patterns of operation and procedures guided by key principles, rules and regulations. These need to be maintained constantly at some minimum level to keep the system alive and functioning. In this regard information helps to make education systems more accountable by providing measures of inputs and outputs as well as trends in performance. These are the essentials that define and maintain any kind of system.

Second, information is essential for policy-making and planning for the future development of education. Policy sets out purpose, goals and objectives for education; planning helps to map out the strategies through which these will be achieved. It is policy and planning which give meaning and life to an education system and enable us to talk about effectiveness and efficiency in education. An effective system is one that delivers what it was designed to achieve; an efficient system is one that makes optimum use of available resources to achieve its goals.

Third, information is essential because it facilitates vital research into various aspects of education by providing raw data on different variables. It is through research that we gain greater insight into the achievements and failures of an education system. Research enables us to understand what is working and what is not, as well as why certain things are the way they are, and how other things can be changed for the better. In due course, research helps us to improve the process of education as well as the education system and its impact on society.

It is essential to understand that in practice, these three key strands which define the essence of information are highly inter-related. Good research contributes to policy and planning for the education system, while sound policies and plans set goals and operating strategies for the system. In a reciprocal way, good management and routine administration ensure effective and efficient implementation of policies and plans, which themselves help to put research findings to the test. The common thread running through this complex inter-relationship is information. That is why technology for improvements in the generation, storage, transmission, processing and retrieval of information is vital for management and development in any education system. *If there is anything worse than a failing education system, it is one in which the managers at various levels are not aware that the system is failing.*

What Kind of Information is Critical?

The kind of information required at different points of the education system depends very much on how centralised or decentralised the system is in practice. It is the degree of decentralisation that determines critical management functions from school level to central ministry level. The management functions in turn determine which kind of information is critical. Most of the information used in the management of education systems originates from individual schools. It is therefore at the school level that we need to encourage a proper understanding of the importance of different kinds of information for the education system. It is critical that teachers and school heads appreciate the usefulness of the information they collect, both for their own purposes as a school and for all other purposes that go beyond the school to district, regional and national levels. The greater a school's autonomy, the more it needs to give careful consideration to its own information needs for decision-making and management purposes. Consideration must also be given to the kind of information that schools are expected to provide for use at other levels – district, region and central Ministry. It is evident that schools need to collect a wide range of information, and may need to review regularly the information collected to determine what is useful to whom, as well as what information they should continue to collect, and for what purpose. In other words, there needs to be a balance between the extent to which information collection is treated as a routine process involving a fixed range of data, and the extent to which it is treated as a dynamic process with regular review of the range of data to be collected.

This balance depends very much on the changing circumstances and realities of the school system. As an education system becomes more decentralised and schools gain a greater degree of autonomy, it is necessary not only to review the range of data routinely collected, and the kind of information needed by the schools, but to review the kind of 'accountability' information through which schools are judged by the community they serve and the central Ministry to which they are also accountable. It may therefore be useful for schools to view the information they collect in terms of data categories that can expand or contract according to prevailing circumstances and information needs. The data categories can then be regarded as relatively fixed, while the actual information collected can be subject to change as the information needs for decision-making change. Table 3.1 (page 84) illustrates the kind of information typically collected in schools, and outlines this in terms of a number of fixed data categories.

In general, the more routine the information requirements, the easier it is for the data collection process to be made simple and routine at the school level. This also means that schools can better handle the data collection and information processing tasks essential for decision-making and management. By the same token, the data that gets to the district and central Ministry levels from the schools becomes more reliable and accurate. The use of technology can play a significant role in promoting these kinds of outcomes, particularly where information requirements can be put in terms of routine data collection and processing to provide standard indicators. Technology can also play a critical role in making changes to the kind of information collected, in order to meet the

Table 3.1 Examples of Information Collected in Schools for Various Data Categories

Data category	Kind of information typically collected at the school level
Access data	Number of learners according to age, gender, locality, and other identifying characteristics (religion, race, tribe, etc.). Some schools also record information on number of applicants as well as on the numbers actually accepted and enrolled in the school.
Attendance data	Daily attendance record indicating lateness, absences, etc., usually in the class attendance register. Some schools record reasons for lateness and absences, which may be useful later for analysis.
Data on pedagogical resources	Number of teachers by age, gender, qualification, training, area of specialisation, experience, seniority, etc. Textbooks, equipment and other teaching and learning aids; the availability and use of in-service training opportunities for teachers may also be recorded.
Data on curriculum delivery	Class size; teaching loads; textbooks; learning aids; number of subjects; pattern of availability; timetable; participation in various subjects; specialist facilities; equipment; consumable materials; pupil contact hours; teaching style (record of work lesson notes).
Data on budgetary inputs (income and expenditure)	Staff salary grants; capitation grants; PTA funds; school fees; other charges; community contributions; proprietor funds, etc.; expenditure on salaries and allowances, pedagogical materials, the maintenance of facilities and equipment, routine supplies, services and overheads, etc.
Data on attainment and performance record	Assessment of learning in terms of continuous work and periodic tests as well as internal promotion examinations and major external examinations. In some cases standardised tests at certain grades may be taken for a large sample of schools. Mark Book data and project work record. Record of promotion, repetition, drop-out. Some schools may also record data on behaviour, sports, drama and other areas of performance outside the academic curriculum.

challenges of changing information requirements at different levels of the education system. However, its use here requires much more careful planning.

How Information Can be Used

Information can be used to promote greater effectiveness and efficiency, as well as to present a picture of the system to decision-makers. In other words, it can be used for measuring inputs, tracking processes and measuring outputs in education. It can also be used to make projections about future requirements, and therefore to aid planning for the development of the system – for example, to project future needs for trained teachers, additional classrooms and pedagogical equipment. Table 3.2 shows some possible uses of information in the education system.

Table 3.2 Examples of Possible Information Use at Different Levels

Category of information	Using information at the school level	Using the information beyond school level
Access data	Level of demand indicated by percentage of applicants enrolled. For high demand a school can decide to make more use of its capacity, or even to expand it, to take in more applicants; to keep enrolment steady in the interest of quality, or to maintain a scarcity that justifies high fees, etc. Dis-aggregated data can also tell if the school is serving its whole community in an equitable manner. Are there far more boys than girls? Is it mainly the rich who get in?, etc.	The distribution pattern of enrolment levels can help to determine policy measures and strategies. Building more schools, expanding existing ones, closing down some small schools, introducing shift systems, using alternative means for delivering education to some groups, etc., are all options that can be taken up as policy depending on what the access data shows for a district, region, or the national system in general.
Attendance data	Can be used to identify learners at risk of dropping out. Poor attendance leads to early drop-out. Also helps identify home/community factors that affect regular school attendance.	Measure of efficiency, since absence and lateness are forms of wastage and reduced learning contact time for the pupils. Indicator of disconsonance between schools and their communities?
Data on pedagogical resources	Can be used to judge how well prepared the school is to meet pupils' learning needs. Also gives a basis for deciding what the school needs to help improve quality.	Can be a basis for deciding on what additional resources and budgets for pedagogy should be allocated to each school. Measure of how 'rich' the schools are in terms of their learning environment. Helps inform decisions on range of new resources required in different categories of schools.
Data on curriculum delivery	Basis for management planning on how best to use available resources for improved delivery of the pre-scribed school curriculum. Deployment of staff, room allocation, equipment use, etc. can all be planned from this data.	Policy on staff deployment, provision of specialist facilities and setting of targets for school achievement can be based on this kind of data.
Data on budgetary inputs	Income and expenditure indicative of the solvency of the school or how far it is being subsidised, and by whom. Measure of efficiency with which available funds are being used.	Policy on funding of schools and how any subsidies should be targeted. Rules of accountability for the funds provided to schools and the fees they may levy on users or communities.
Performance record data	Indicator of how well the school is doing in serving its clients.	Performance league table. Basis for additional assistance to some schools and for demanding improvements in others.

Overview of Current Practices

Using Technology to Improve Management

In their country papers on education and technology, prepared for the 13CCEM, most countries indicated that technology was being used mainly in connection with education management. The main focus in this regard is on computerisation and the setting up of an efficient EMIS. Many countries have made good progress in terms of computerisation, which has enabled them to produce more reliable and current educational statistics. Despite this progress there is still a very ambivalent attitude towards the use of technology for management of education institutions and systems. In some countries it seems that the introduction of computers in itself is regarded as a progressive step in managing education systems. There is often a striking lack of a coherent strategy and comprehensive plan for using technology to improve educational management. This seems partly due to *ad hoc* decisions made about investing in different technologies at various times, under the influence of commercial companies or as part of projects sponsored by external agencies. Such projects may involve provision of computers and training of staff in specific areas such as educational statistics or sector analysis, but they are not fully integrated into the general educational management process. Similarly, at the school level some institutions succeed in obtaining one or two computers for record keeping and data processing, as part of school management. In other countries, there are impressive developments with systematic attempts to plan and create an EMIS.

Addressing the Challenges

In general, challenges relating to the use of technology for education management can be encountered at the information collection stage as well as in processing, storage, and use of information. The key objectives in using technology efficiently in this area can be summarised as follows:

- move towards a once-only recording or input of data wherever possible;
- increase reliable storage and easy retrieval of data by authorised persons, while restricting the risk of unauthorised access to sensitive information;
- promote easy transfer of data to every point in the system at which it may be needed for management decisions, while minimising the risk of data corruption in transit; and
- promote rapid, accurate and reliable processing of information through the use of standard techniques, procedures and programmes.

In order to meet these objectives, the various challenges at each stage of the information chain must be addressed.

Collection Challenges

The main challenge relating to the collection of information for EMIS is to overcome the inefficiency of repetition (the same information has to be provided at different times and in different places), while avoiding the restriction of time and place for valid data collection. The two main implications of this challenge are that:

1 Any data or information required should preferably be collected and entered into the system once only. Thereafter it should be accessible whenever and wherever it is required in the system, without having to be collected again or re-entered. This is where modern IT offers definite advantages over the old manual data collection and record-keeping systems.
2 Data and information required should preferably be collected and entered into the system from a variety of places and at various times, in order to avoid bottlenecks and other restrictions of time and place.

In addition, it is of course essential to ensure that the information has been collected with due care and diligence by staff who understand the value of accuracy and reliability in collecting information.

Processing and Storage Challenges

Since information is processed differently for different purposes, the main challenge in this area is the need for flexibility and versatility in handling data processing. The use of standard techniques and procedures in data processing is important for rapid and reliable results. It is also important that data processing is programmed to take account of the information needs at various points in the system. All of this can best be achieved when clearly defined indicators are used, together with standard methods of calculating such indicators from well-specified raw data. The use of computers makes it possible to produce a wide range of indicators through rapid processing of raw data collected and entered into the system. This eliminates the risk of human error in the processing of information, and reduces the problem of long delays due to manual calculations and processing.

However, even with computers problems can arise – for example, when all the raw data is not available in the standard form necessary for calculating a particular indicator. In such situations human judgement comes into play – in deciding how to process the raw data at hand in order to obtain useful results. It is also important to appreciate that despite the high speed and accuracy of computer processing, the results are only as reliable and useful as the original raw data used to make the calculations.

In terms of information storage, the main challenge is to ensure that those who need the information can have ready access to it, while safeguarding it from those not authorised to access it. Electronic data bases are the ultimate means of storage and data files are generally made 'read only' so that the information they contain can be accessed and used but not changed by those who are not responsible for processing the data. With any data storage system it is important to have back-up copies of the data files in case of accidents, and this is easier to do for electronic files than for hard records.

Utilisation Challenges

At one level the use of information in education management is fairly routine and straightforward. It can give us a picture of current reality regarding the size of the education system (how many learners and staff at each level); the cost of the system in terms of salaries, supplies, maintenance, etc.; and the quality of the system as regards examination results and promotion rates.

At another level, insight, judgement and vision are part of the key to proper utilisation of information in education. This level entails going beyond the indicators and trying to read further meaning into the data as a basis for action or decision-making. This applies at the national as well as local levels, where proper utilisation of information involves a blend of quantitative and qualitative information to guide action, planning and decision-making.

At yet another level, information is used in education management for making projections and predictions on the future impact of some new policy or plan for the education system. In this regard good modelling via the computer can play a key role in rapidly plotting different future scenarios based on current data and some assumptions about the future.

Formulating Policies and Strategies

EMIS Policy

It is commendable that many Commonwealth countries now have a strong desire to establish (or enhance) an educational management information system. For many developing countries this move towards an efficient EMIS has served as the main rationale for introducing computers into the education system. In this regard it is fair to say that some countries have faced a dilemma over the introduction and use of computers for EMIS. Among the issues they have had to consider are how many computers are necessary; where they should be located; whether (and how) they should be linked; what software packages to invest in, and who should be trained to use and access them. For some countries matters have been complicated by the *ad hoc* approach they have been obliged to take in this important policy area, because of pressures from various projects and commercial agents.

In principle there are two broad strategies for introducing computerisation as part of an efficient EMIS. The first is to start with computerisation at the central or Ministry level, and move the process outwards to the regional or provincial level, then to the district or zone level, and finally to the level of the school. This strategy tends to be preferred in the more centralised education systems where the focus is on producing national-level information for management of the system. It is also an attractive option for some countries in the sense that it requires relatively fewer computers and training for a small number of staff. Computerisation can therefore be introduced in a phased and affordable manner. However, this strategy is feasible only if the flow of quality information from the other levels to the central Ministry is timely, reliable and efficient. This can be promoted through the use of other communications technology such as fax machines. If the infrastructure exists, schools can fax information directly to the central Ministry. At least it may be feasible for schools to forward information to the district or regional office, from where it may be possible to fax through to the central Ministry.

The second strategy is to encourage computerisation at the school level, so that the required information can be collected and processed in a more efficient manner, and made available speedily to those who need it. This strategy means that information can be provided in electronic form by the school, thereby eliminating the need to re-enter it at various points, and reducing the risk of human error which this implies.

Beyond these two broad strategies, computerisation can be extended or deepened in other ways to benefit the education system. For instance, school links can be promoted within a country as well as internationally, to encourage exchange of ideas between teachers, students and administrators, as well as to compare management information and other vital indicators of the education system. It is also possible to promote local area networks (LANs) that link local schools to each other and to the district office. The ultimate would be a national network linking all schools to each other and to all relevant education centres through a national grid, like the one proposed for Britain.

Improved Technology

Deciding on improvements to the technology used for education management information systems involves difficult choices. Given the reality of what obtains in the average school in most developing Commonwealth countries, it may not be feasible to do away with the basic manual record-keeping systems currently in place. However, even in the most deprived schools, the use of simple battery or solar-powered programmable calculators can make a world of difference. This simple technology can increase the speed at which indicators are calculated from raw data, and improve the reliability of information provided by the school by reducing human error in the processing of data. Moreover, such calculators are now so cheap that they are easily affordable even for poor schools.

Schools and countries that cannot afford wholesale computerisation can take a gradual approach to improving transmission technology. Where a fax machine already exists at school or district level, and it is not yet possible to provide a computer, the school data can be faxed to a centre where it can be entered into a computer. The general principle is that making use of whatever level of technology is currently available, and improving on it in a gradual way, depending on what is affordable. It is not necessary to wait until all the latest and most appropriate technologies are available at all levels before embarking on the task of developing an efficient EMIS for the country.

Staff Training

It is important to be realistic about staff training and to have a clear idea of which staff need to be trained in which aspect of information technology. In principle, once the standard data to be collected has been determined and the forms designed, it is possible for fairly junior staff to be rapidly trained to enter the data into a computer. However, manual collation of such data (where there is no computer) needs to be handled by a higher level of staff. In both cases careful supervision of the process by senior staff is required, in order to be able to vouch for the accuracy and integrity of the information provided. Usually, fairly senior educational planners have responsibility for the design of data collection instruments or forms, and these are sent to the schools and other data collection points. The planners need to provide adequate training for staff at the school level who are responsible for collecting and sending the information to them. In terms of data collection then, the important area of staff training concerns the education planners who design the instruments and forms. Beyond this actual collection of the information is a routine responsibility that teachers and other staff carry out with only basic training.

Where computers are not available at the school or district levels, staff training is needed for processing the information to produce the standard indicators and other statistics required. Where computers are available, staff must be trained to use software for processing the information. In more sophisticated systems it may be necessary to train computer programmers who can develop or customise specific programmes for processing educational information.

The most important area of staff training needs is in the utilisation of information for decision-making and management at all levels. School heads should be in a position to supervise the collection of information and vouch for its accuracy and integrity. More importantly, they should be able to use such information for the decision-making and management processes necessary to operating a good school. This area of training is of great significance, particularly in decentralised education systems. In much the same way, education planners at district level need to be properly trained in how to use data for decision-making and management of the sub-system for which they have responsibility. Beyond this, senior planners at the central Ministry level need to be well trained in using data to guide policy-making and modelling for the system, as well as to provide the standard descriptive and analytical accounts for education in the country as a whole.

Case Study 3: The Use of Information Technology for the Management of Education in Singapore

Dr Christina Soh

Information Management Research Centre

Nanyang Business School, Nanyang Technological University, Singapore

The Singapore Education System

In order to understand the use of information technology (IT) in the management of education, it is necessary to have and overview of the key features of the Singapore education system.

The Ministry of Education (MOE) plays a central role in directing and formulating the implementation of education policies. It controls the development and administration of primary and secondary schools and junior colleges. The administrative load is significant, given that there are 193 primary schools, 147 secondary schools and 14 junior colleges. The average number of students per school is about 1,500.

Students take national examinations at several points in their school career. MOE is responsible for processing examination results and for determining the posting of students to schools. The first nation-wide examination taken by students is the Primary School Leaving Examination (PSLE), after six years of primary school education. Based on the results of these examinations, MOE streams students into the Special, Express or Normal secondary-school streams, and posts students to schools. Students in the Special and Express courses sit for the GCE 'O' level exam at the end of their four-year course. The Normal course offers a four-year programme leading to the GCE 'N' level exam. A fifth year is available to students who do well in this exam, to enable them to prepare for and take the GCE 'O' level exam.

MOE co-ordinates the GCE examinations and grading processes, and posts students to junior colleges, centralised institutes, polytechnics, or institutes of technical education, based on their results and preferences. Junior college and centralised institute students go on to sit for their GCE 'A' level examinations after two and three years respectively.

MOE also employs about 23,000 teachers and it hopes to recruit an additional 3,000 in 1998–99. MOE is responsible for interviewing and recruiting new teachers; arranging for their training at the National Institute of Education; posting them to schools; arranging courses for continuing professional education, and maintaining personnel records for payroll and promotion.

The schools focus on the delivery of education and the development of students. The management activities at school level include maintaining student records; school-level examination administration; scheduling classes; management of school facilities, equipment and library resources, and management of teaching and administrative staff. The management of each school is performed by the principal, with the assistance of a vice-principal, school administrator, and a few clerical staff and non-teaching staff. The latter

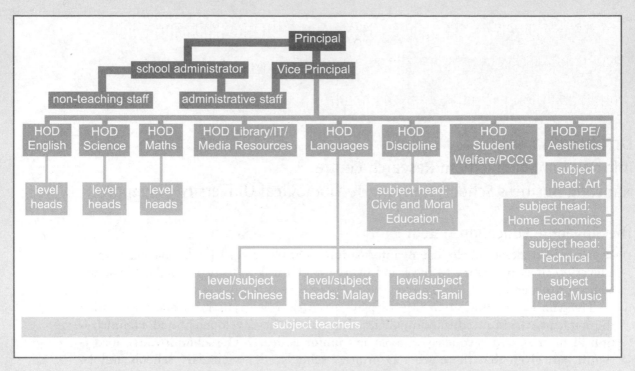

Figure 3.1 The Organisation of Primary Schools in Singapore (may vary from school to school)

provide support in areas such as IT, and in science laboratories. The management of academic content, within the curriculum set by MOE, is performed by heads of departments. The typical management structure of schools is shown in Figures 3.1–3.4.

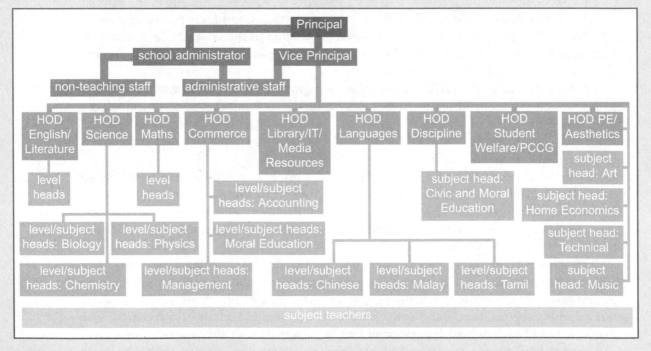

Figure 3.2 The Organisation of Secondary Schools in Singapore (may vary from school to school)

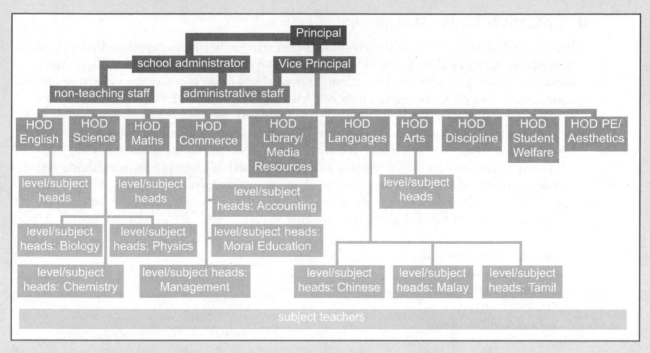

Figure 3.3 The Organisation of Junior Colleges in Singapore (may vary from JC to JC)

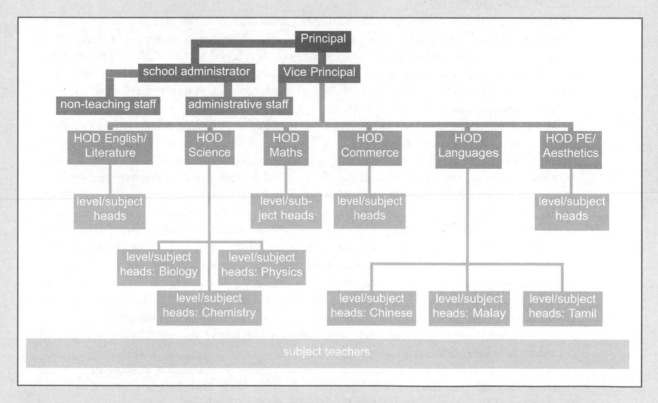

Figure 3.4 The Organisation of Centralised Institutes in Singapore (may vary from CI to CI)

IT Applications for the Management of Education

The centralisation of examinations, student posting, teacher recruitment and personnel data placed a heavy data processing burden on MOE. Computerisation of these areas therefore began in 1979, on a minicomputer platform. The focus was on creating and maintaining data on students, teachers and schools. By 1984 MOE had moved to a mainframe, using the ADABAS database system. Also in the mid-1980s, school systems were developed and installed. These were DOS-based, on stand-alone microcomputers. Most of these have now been replaced with client-server systems linked to MOE.

Today there are over 100 applications in the portfolio of systems supporting the management of education. The majority of these are mainframe systems, with newer applications on the client-server platform. The portfolio of applications can be logically categorised into the following major functional areas:

- examination systems;
- student posting systems;
- personnel systems;
- financial systems; and
- school-level systems.

Each of the categories is presented below in terms of major system functionality and user groups, impacts, training issues and challenges to implementation and operation. Where applicable, plans are outlined for significant new systems.

Examination Systems

MOE examination systems cover the national examinations at the end of primary school, secondary school and junior college/pre-university. The majority of the examination systems are currently mainframe-based and were developed in the 1980s. The systems face the usual legacy system issues such as difficulty of maintenance and lack of proper system documentation. They have therefore undergone a major review and steps to develop new systems have already begun.

Major administrative tasks related to examinations are student registration, examination logistics, and processing of results. The examination system obtains data on all students who are eligible to take the national examination from the MOE student database. This minimises the need for data entry during the examination registration process. For the GCE 'O', 'N' and 'A' level examinations, government school students fill in an OMR (Optical Magnetic Reader) form, which is checked by school teachers and sent to MOE for processing. Private candidates register via the Internet. MOE prints lists of examination candidates and sends them to schools to verify. Examination logistics include nominating examiners and markers, and scheduling classrooms and laboratories for the examinations. Nomination of examiners and markers is done manually at schools, and the information is sent to MOE for data entry. MOE has computerised information on school laboratories, and the scheduling of these is computerised.

MOE examination systems also generate barcode labels for identifying batches of completed examination scripts, saving examiners administrative time and increasing data entry accuracy during the processing of results. The examination results processing systems also update the student database. Results slips and lists are generated and printed at MOE and sent to schools for handing out to students.

The review of the examination systems includes a redesign of the examination administrative process so that all national examinations will follow the same streamlined process. This will allow examination branch personnel at MOE to handle enquiries and tasks across the various national examinations. The redesigned process will include internet registrations for all candidates. One of the main challenges in implementing the new system will be to change the mindset of personnel so that cross-functional work is accepted. Singapore has a unique examination structure, which means that no suitable package application can be found, and a vendor will have to develop the system. Where possible, however, packages will be incorporated. For example, the new examination system will incorporate a software package for examination scheduling.

Posting Students to Schools

Major posting exercises are conducted each year for children entering Primary 1, Secondary 1, junior colleges, polytechnics and institutes of education (ITE). Primary 1 registration and posting involves over 40,000 students each year. The process has been computerised so that very little data entry is required when teachers register each child at the school. Teachers need only enter the child's birth certificate number, and all personal particulars of the child are retrieved from a centralised on-line file created from data on the year's cohort of six-year-olds. This data is obtained from the Ministry of Home Affairs. Registration is done in phases, the early phases being reserved for those with sibling, old-boy and other ties to the school, and proximity to home.

Computerisation has provided significant benefits to parents, who need only make one quick visit to a school to register their child. The number of vacancies in each school is determined quickly and posted on the MOE web site within a day or two after each phase. This information is eagerly sought by parents who have not yet secured a place for their child in the school of their choice, as it helps them to estimate the likelihood of enrolling their child in a later registration phase. A further advantage is that school administrators no longer have to physically transport the registration data to MOE for processing at the end of each registration day.

MOE posts primary school students to secondary schools based on their PSLE examination results (obtained in computerised form from the examinations system) and their preferences for various secondary schools. Students indicate their preferences for up to six secondary schools on a manual form; teachers verify then enter this information on-line. Data entry effort is minimised because relevant student information is retrieved on-line from MOE during the data entry process.

Secondary students who have taken the GCE examinations indicate their preferences for specific junior colleges, polytechnics and ITEs. They are given the option of entering their preferences on-line to MOE via the internet, or submitting the information to their teachers who will enter it for them. Results of the posting are printed by MOE and sent to schools to hand to students. The posting results can also be accessed via the internet.

Teacher training requirements have been low because these systems are easy to use. For the Primary 1 registration system, two teachers per school were nominated to attend an MOE half-day, hands-on training course prior to the rollout. In subsequent years, only briefings were necessary. For the posting systems to Secondary 1, junior colleges, polytechnics and ITEs, no hands-on training was necessary as the systems were simple data entry screens, and the teachers did not have to interact with the public during data entry. Any queries could be handled by calling the help-desk.

The major challenges for these on-line posting systems were to provide sufficient line and processing capacity to ensure acceptable response times at schools during registration periods. This is critical for Primary 1 registration which requires the presence of parents. The response time issue was handled by giving the registration and posting systems priority in use of network and processing resources. Back-up plans were made in case line-drop problems occurred. For the launch of internet applications for posting, MOE assessment of usage based on the size of the student cohort led it to lease the use of a commercial internet provider's server for the duration of the posting exercise.

Personnel Systems

All personnel systems reside on the mainframe at MOE. At the heart of these systems is the teacher data bank containing information about teachers from the point of recruitment onwards. It includes data on qualifications, work experience, and staff confidential evaluations. The main systems that access and update the teacher data bank are the appointment systems for new employees; the teacher posting system that posts teachers to schools, and the confirmation and bar systems which process teacher promotions. The personnel system interfaces with the government-wide system for payroll processing.

At present, data is input to these systems at MOE. For example, when a teacher graduates from training at the National Institute of Education, a manual form is raised, and sent to MOE for data entry to create a new record for the teacher. Subsequently, whenever a teacher is posted to a different school, a form is raised for MOE data entry to update the teacher's record. When a teacher takes a course, the school submits an occurrence form to MOE to update the teacher's training record. Challenges of the current systems are heavy data entry load; complexities in update from multiple sources, and synchronisation of the database.

However, the personnel systems have resulted in a very rich teacher database. Routine and management reports are prepared from data extracted from this database, for MOE decision-makers. For example, the annual exercise of posting teachers to schools uses data such as the teacher's qualifications, experience and place of residence. (The last helps MOE to place teachers in schools near their homes where possible.) Management reviews of teacher-student complement, which assess whether schools have an acceptable student-teacher ratio, also draw data from the teacher database and combine it with data from the student database.

A major review is planned for personnel systems in the latter part of 1998. There are already plans to provide schools with on-line access to training systems, and to relieve teacher management systems. The on-line training system will be an intranet system that teachers can access even from home. It will allow them to plan their individual training, which will be approved by supervisory staff. The systems will also provide course directories that teachers can access. Teachers will be able to nominate themselves for courses, and their nominations will be routed by the system to supervisory staff for approval. Teachers will also be able to provide feedback on the training they receive. Training co-ordinators in each school will also use the system to provide consolidated training plans and records for the school as a whole.

The other school-level personnel system is for managing relief teachers. Relief teachers are often engaged directly by schools, hence school administrators require on-line access to the relief teacher management system to input personnel data for payroll processing.

Financial Systems

A major new system recently implemented in all schools is the Integrated Financial Accounting and Administrative System (IFAAS). This system is on the client-server platform and provides schools with on-line access to MOE. The client application at the school level is used by school administrators to prepare budgets, and to post purchase orders and collections of miscellaneous fees. IFAAS also serves the various departments at MOE, who use it for budgeting, raising purchase orders, and initiating payments. The MOE finance department uses IFAAS to consolidate the budget, to process payments centrally for all schools and MOE departments, and to check school and MOE departmental expenditure against budgets. The system also interfaces with the Ministry of Finance.

One major impact of this system has been the centralisation of payments processing, resulting in much faster issuance of cheques to suppliers. In addition, wherever possible, suppliers are paid via electronic funds transfer. All schools' power and telecommunications bills are also paid electronically. The system has reduced payment-related administrative work in schools.

The training of users for this system was a challenge because there were about five users in each of the 360 schools, as well as 200 users at MOE. The users at the school level were the principal, school administrator and clerks. Each user was provided with two days hands-on training, conducted by a vendor engaged by MOE. Training focused not only on system use, but on basic financial and budgeting concepts. Another challenge was installation of the client application in all 360 schools, which required significant IT manpower.

School-Level Systems

Since 1986 schools have had stand-alone, DOS-based microcomputer administration systems for capturing student data and managing the library. These have been replaced by a new suite of school-level applications which are Windows-based, and which allow direct data transfer between schools and MOE. This is possible because all schools now have at least an administration local area network with five microcomputers, and a leased line link to MOE. All schools also have internet access and internet accounts for teachers. Efforts are under way to upgrade the IT infrastructure at schools for both instructional and administrative purposes. These will be discussed below (page 101, The Master Plan for IT in Education). The new school-level systems are:

· student management systems: All student data is sent on-line to the school once the students have been posted to the school. From then on, the school keeps the student records updated with information such as classes, extra-curricular activities and examination results. The system also enables teachers to capture and print examination results slips. The student management system periodically transfers data up to MOE to update the central student database.
· student profiling system: For use in pastoral care and career guidance, it also stores student profiles with information on academic performance and extra-curricular activities, and family background. Counselling and interview notes can also be stored in the profiles.
· physical fitness testing: Stores and analyses students' height, weight and physical fitness test data.

These systems were implemented in 1997, and are relatively new. Initial impacts include more timely data transfer about students between schools and MOE, although some teachers find data entry difficult as they are not comfortable with microcomputers.

User training during the rollout of the systems to schools was heavy because all teachers needed to interact with the student management systems. MOE is attempting to alleviate the on-going training burden by disseminating a user guide and FAQs (frequently asked questions) on the MOE-schools intranet.

Some challenges arose initially during the rollout because the systems assume a standard process at schools. However, schools have some discretion when implementing various MOE guidelines and this sometimes results in differing processes at schools.

This section has provided a functional view of the key systems in education management, and system-specific discussion of impacts, user training and challenges. The following sections will give an overview of key training and support issues, and impacts.

User Training and Support

One clear implication of the move to on-line access for schools is the increase in the number of users who have to be trained. For mainframe systems with no on-line access by schools, only a small number of MOE users needed to be trained. However, the number of users increases dramatically when the systems are rolled out to schools, as with the school-level student management system, and the Integrated Financial Accounting and Administrative System. MOE has dealt with the increased training burden in a number of ways:

· out-sourcing training to the vendor;
· making user interfaces as easy as possible, so that minimal or no user training is required. This was possible for the primary registration system, and the GCE student posting systems for selection of school preferences;
· planning to move towards web-based training, making training material available on the intranet;
· having on-site technical assistants at each primary school, and access to help-desk support for secondary schools. The help-desk is operated by a vendor that MOE has appointed to provide support to schools. The on-site technical assistants are also employees of the vendor. MOE initially provides some applications-specific training to the technical assistants, but the vendor is responsible for ensuring that the knowledge is subsequently transmitted to new vendor employees.

In addition to the application-specific training for the relevant users each time a new system is rolled out, MOE provided all 23,000 teachers with two days of basic training in Word and internet. A smaller number of teachers received additional training in Excel and PowerPoint. The training was done by vendors and took about a year.

The Major Impacts of IT

The major impacts of the use of IT for education management are efficiency and accuracy; convenience for users, and better information for decision-making and planning. These are summarised, with examples, in Table 3.3.

Table 3.3 The Major Impacts of IT Systems for Management of Education in Singapore

Functional Category	Major System Impacts
Examination systems	**Efficiency and accuracy:**
	• Minimises data entry of student particulars
	• Accurate processing of examination results
	• Generation of results slips for schools
	Convenience:
	• Any time, anywhere, internet registration for GCE examinations
	• On-line access to results for private candidates
Student posting systems	**Efficiency and accuracy:**
	• Minimises data entry of student particulars
	• Sharply reduced Primary 1 registration time for parents
	• No need for principals to transport Primary 1 registration data to MOE at the end of each phase
	• Greater accuracy in matching students' school preferences with eligibility as determined by results
	Convenience:
	• Any time, anywhere, internet selection of students' school preferences
	• On-line access to results of posting
Personnel systems	**Better information for decision-making:**
	• Teacher database provides information for posting and promotions, as well as for policy-making
	• Intranet teacher training system supports individual training, road-map planning, course nomination and evaluation
Financial systems	**Efficiency and accuracy:**
	• Less payment administration at schools, due to computerisation and centralisation of payment processing
	• Faster payment settlement with less labour due to electronic funds transfer
School-level systems	**Better information for decision-making:**
	• More up-to-date student information captured at schools, and updated at MOE
	• Easily accessible student information available, for pastoral care and career counselling
	Efficiency and accuracy:
	• Minimises data entry of student data at schools and HQ

Time and labour savings arise from providing schools with on-line access to MOE data. This removes the need for a great deal of manual recording of data. School administrators and teachers usually need only to verify the student data retrieved on-line and to input only minimal additional update data. MOE staff are also relieved of data entry when schools are given access to update school, teacher and student data themselves.

Convenience for school staff, students and parents is also evident from systems that have moved on-line. Intranet and internet-based systems in particular provide users with any time, anywhere access.

Finally, the rich computer databases that have been built up on students, teachers and schools provide timely and comprehensive information for MOE decision-makers, as well as for school principals and senior school administrators.

Future Directions: The Master Plan for IT in Education

Recently implemented systems and planned systems clearly show the following trends:

- on-line information access and update, providing users (school staff, students and parents) with anytime, anywhere access to relevant data such as school postings and examination results;
- use of client-server, internet and intranet platforms;
- electronic funds payment for schools and MOE expenses, and collection of fees;
- streamlining and standardising administrative processes with the help of IT; and
- web-based training and user support.

The Master Plan for IT in Education, which was approved in early 1997, will provide a further boost to these trends. The Master Plan is focused primarily on establishing IT-based teaching and learning in schools. However, the human and physical infrastructure that will be put in place to promote learning objectives will have a positive spill-over effect on education management and administration also.

In terms of human infrastructure, the plan will require teachers to use educational software in teaching, and to access web sites for educational content. This will pave the way for launching computer applications in more areas of education management, particularly those that can be deployed using web-based technology. The plan foresees that internal e-mail will be the dominant mode of communication between MOE and schools, and among teachers in various schools. To achieve this, a comprehensive training plan is in place with heads of departments and selected teachers being trained, and they in turn will train other teachers.

The number of microcomputers in schools is being increased so that primary schools will have a student to computer ratio of 6.6 to 1, and secondary schools and junior colleges will have a ratio of 5 to 1. The ready access to computers in schools will allow students to do more data entry themselves, for example examination registration. All students from Primary 4 and above will have internet accounts. Teachers will have notebooks, and this computing portability will open up new ways to access and update information any time, anywhere. All schools will receive whole-school networks, which will be linked to a wide area network. This, in turn, will be connected eventually to a high-speed national backbone.

The Master Plan for IT in Education is a blueprint for the integration of IT in education. Twenty-two demo schools have already been provided with the physical infrastructure and training, and have begun to experiment with the use of IT throughout the curriculum. The rollout to all schools is scheduled for completion in 2002. It is a serious and ambitious effort to enrich the learning environment; encourage creative thinking; innovate pedagogy, and promote administrative and management excellence. The use of IT for management education, as reviewed in this case study, will be continually reviewed and renewed as the Master Plan unfolds in the next five years.

Note

I should like to thank the IT personnel at MOE who participated in the preparation of this case study. They contributed their time and their considerable knowledge of IT use in the Singapore education system.

4 Technology for Quality Learning and Teaching

Understanding the Issues

It would not be an exaggeration to argue that most teaching and learning aids are largely extensions and enhancements of the basic face-to-face method of education. In a conventional school setting, these aids promote greater effectiveness and efficiency within the finite real-time encounters of face-to-face learning situations. How can one teach the history of a foreign country in two 40-minute periods, or complex mathematical theorems in three lessons? The answer, if we are talking about effective teaching and learning, has to include the use of aids. This concept of 'aids' should remind us that they are in a sense supplementary to the fundamental process of teaching and learning, which involves a process of engaging minds and opening up avenues for exploration and discovery. This process generally involves such acts as providing information; explaining concepts; illustrating principles; giving examples; outlining procedures; demonstrating processes; advancing arguments; highlighting points; asking questions; giving feedback; exchanging ideas; and performing tasks. Fundamental and most central to this process is talking and communicating through language. It is this that is augmented in various ways by the teaching and learning aids used in education. Therefore, even the best aids cannot be a substitute for a good teacher. Human communication is central to the process of learning. To the extent that technology can facilitate and enhance such communication it has the potential to improve pedagogy and the quality of education.

This is not to argue for a teacher-centred view of education, nor to deny that people can, and do, learn on their own. The intention is simply to highlight the important role of the teacher at a time when we are too easily tempted to believe that advances in technology are eroding the importance of the teacher's role in education. The reality is that the teacher's role is changing significantly, but it remains fundamental to what we call education. The explosion of knowledge and information over the past few decades has meant that teachers can no longer be viewed as the source of all that the learner needs to know. However, mere availability of knowledge and information should not be confused with the process of education. It is essential that learners are initiated into the ways of understanding and making use of the available knowledge and information. This is what lies at the heart of good teaching. On this basis it can be argued that the greatest success of any teacher is to help create an autonomous learner – one who can go on learning alone long after the teacher has 'withdrawn' from the process.

The collection of books in any library does not constitute knowledge as such. It is only with the guidance of the teacher and the development of certain skills by the learner, that the collection can become a source of information and knowledge to be mined by the learner. Similarly, the vast amount of information on the internet, or the world-wide web, does not in itself constitute knowledge. It is only to the extent that learners know what to do with such information that we can begin to talk about it as knowledge, as distinct from mere information. This entails much more than simply knowing how to access information on the web. It is important to reiterate that learning is primarily the responsibility of the learner, and that the teacher's role is that of 'tour guide' on the magical exploration of the world of knowledge. It is equally important to remind ourselves that without this kind of guidance provided by the teacher, most learners would flounder on the vast and infinitely complex web of information and knowledge that is available in the modern world.

So what are the key professional attributes that enable teachers to perform the crucial role for learning and education to take place? In a word, much of it is about good pedagogy. Parents, peers and many other people facilitate learning by various means. What is special about the teaching profession is that it makes the most intensive and systematic use of pedagogy to promote effective and efficient learning as part of the process of education. Teachers are expected to be experts at promoting and facilitating learning. In order to do so they need a comprehensive bank of pedagogical skills and teaching aids. Many would argue that in addition they need certain personal qualities that enable them to engage learners in the process that results in education. For instance, it is vital for teachers to be able to attract the attention of learners, and to hold their interest on a sustained basis, as well as to win their trust and respect. The personal qualities that enable teachers to achieve this are very important, and it is not surprising that some people argue that 'good teachers are born not trained'. Be that as it may, the essence of professionalism is that good teachers do not simply provide learners with information or guide the learning process. They inspire learners and help to bring out hidden talents and latent abilities that would otherwise lie dormant. They help to shape perceptions, cultivate attitudes and values, and change behaviours and habits. In sometimes quite remarkable and fundamental ways, good teachers change the lives of many of the learners in their charge! As the saying goes, 'no one forgets a good teacher'.

It is a truism that, given enough time and resources, anyone can be a teacher. This has more to do with the fact that learning comes naturally to human beings (often against great odds), and less to do with any innate teaching abilities we may all possess. It can be argued that in many developing countries the teaching profession has suffered from this phenomenon through which learning is an integral part of human nature. It is one of the few major professions in which governments have easily made do with a high proportion of unqualified and untrained practitioners. It is also a profession that many people have all too readily treated as a 'holding area' in which they can be gainfully employed while trying to qualify for another profession. These unfortunate trends have often resulted in much bad teaching being endured within the education systems of some Commonwealth countries. Policies and strategies relating to the use of technology for improving pedagogy and quality in education should not only support the good teachers, but also help to change bad teaching. This implies an urgent need for continuous professional self-development on the part of all teachers.

So far this brief introduction has explored the nature of good pedagogy; outlined the place of teaching and learning aids in the educational process; highlighted the central role of the teacher, and affirmed the ultimate responsibility of the learner in the process that results in education. A final issue which needs to be touched on, is that of the organisational practice that results in education taking place in formal institutions called schools. It needs to be emphasised that education can and does take place outside such institutions. So what attributes of the school are critical for good pedagogy and quality education, and how can technology enable us to strengthen these attributes within the school as well as to reproduce them in other educational settings outside the school? Conversely, we need to take full cognisance of those attributes of schools which inhibit or impede good pedagogy and good quality in education.

Schools and other educational institutions are different from information centres or learning centres. They do not simply make information available, or provide a space within which learning can take place. As Malcolm Skilbeck expressed it in Botswana, 'schools are places to be'. That is why we talk of schools as having a culture and an ethos, as well as a mission and a curriculum. Over the years schools have been credited, among other things, with a socialising function as well as with the economic role of preparing learners for the world of work. It can be argued, of course, that other social institutions, such as religious bodies and training centres, also perform some of the functions attributed to schools. What is unique about schools is the scale and intensity of the manner in which they perform these functions.

Given an intake of learners, often from diverse backgrounds and of different abilities, schools create a community within which these learners can be properly prepared for a multiplicity of roles in society. It is in this community that perceptions are shaped; principles learnt; values acquired, and relationships formed. Here the emotions are mastered; characters built; behaviour practised, and identities created. Also, and most importantly, it is in this community that learners acquire the life skills that will make them creative and productive members of society. These skills range from basic literacy and numeracy, through mastery of the wide range of forms of human knowledge that are in the curriculum, to pre-vocational, practical and extra-curricula skills. As a community, schools also provide society with what is still the most practical means of transmitting its most cherished values and preferred way of life to the next generation. Because learners constitute a kind of captive clientele, schools can and do provide a very intense and sustained initiation into the norms and values of the society.

However, the organisational principles of the formal school are not always conducive to good pedagogy and quality education. Grouping learners into grades, based ostensibly on age, and expecting each cohort to progress through the system at the same pace can sometimes be counter-productive. Learners of different abilities and from different backgrounds may need to be taught in different ways, and will progress at a different pace from each other. Most teaching targets the average learner, and does not do justice to the slow learner or the fast learner. Similarly, the non-negotiable structure and rather inflexible sequencing of a prescribed curriculum means that most learners cannot learn what they want, when they want, and therefore cannot take full responsibility for their own learning. The constraint of time and place involved in school attendance also means that learners often have to make tough decisions about investment of their time in the learning process, in preference to other activities which may be more critical at that point in their lives. Full time schooling shuts out almost everything else! In a sense also, the school is often separated from the community and the wider society, so that there is a kind of isolation from reality that hinders experiential learning. These weaknesses are often tackled successfully in less formal educational settings. It is also the case that progressive schools and good teachers tend to have their own battery of organisational practices and pedagogical skills for overcoming these difficulties.

The issue is that while many functions, including teaching and learning, can be performed outside the formal school setting, we must not lose sight of the totality of what schools offer in terms of being a 'one-stop' socialising and life-skills development community. At the same time, schools tend to pay a high price for this function in terms of rigid structures, inflexible learning sequences and constraints of time and place for learning. There is much value in a holistic, 'one-stop' community for education, yet there is also much value in the diversity and flexibility that is possible outside the formal school setting. In what ways can technology help us to choose wisely and hold things together as we seek to improve the quality of education within our schools as well as in alternative settings outside schools?

The Fundamentals of Quality in Education

Quality in education is characterised by the three important dimensions of relevance, effectiveness and efficiency. The dimension of relevance highlights the fact that, in practice, quality is not a neutral or absolute concept. It involves valuing, and this is something that different people or communities do differently. Quality is therefore always perceived in relation to something that is valued and desirable in a given context. In this sense, relevance has to be seen not only as pertaining to what is familiar, or what fits in a given context, but also as what relates to the perceived and latent needs of a community of learners, as well as their own hopes and aspirations. All of this helps to shape the curriculum and determine how it is interpreted in various parts of the education system. In this regard quality starts with good curriculum design that takes into account the following components of relevance:

- appropriate forms of knowledge in terms of subjects or disciplines;
- national priorities, goals and objectives that relate to education;
- international issues and concerns that have implications for education;
- local priorities and concerns that relate to education;
- background realities and defining characteristics of the learners; and
- hopes and aspirations for the future (learners, communities and nation).

But even with the best curriculum, the quality of education depends ultimately on how teachers handle what is prescribed for learners. Teachers are responsible for making a curriculum come alive for learners; for helping them to relate to prescribed learning experiences in ways that will useful for them, and for inspiring them with a vision of what they can become on the basis of the curriculum. To carry out this important function teachers need to make maximum use of teaching and learning aids and various forms of technology. The key issue, therefore, is how technology can help us to improve the relevance of education in different settings and localities, when we are dealing with a prescribed curriculum that is often national rather than local.

Effectiveness is about achieving the goals and objectives prescribed in the curriculum, as well as those set for the school itself. This is where good pedagogy is most important, and where we need to be most clear about learning objectives. What is usually advocated is that these objectives should be stated in such a way that we can measure the extent to which they have been achieved at the end of a certain period of time. We rely heavily on tests and examinations to measure learners' performance, and this in turn tells us something about how far the objectives have been achieved at the end of the prescribed period. The important issue here is how to use technology to improve learners' performance, and hence the effectiveness of the educational process. Given what we currently know about how people learn, how best can we use the kind of technologies that we have in order to enhance the learning process? It is likely that we should include greater provision for self-learning; improved access to information and knowledge sources, and more teaching and learning aids in the classroom. All of this implies using technology more intensively to enhance the role of the teacher as the key facilitator of the educational process, while strengthening the role of the learner as the person with central responsibility for learning achievement.

Efficiency is about optimum use of resources to achieve the goals and objectives that are prescribed in a relevant curriculum. It is about cost-effectiveness and value for money, but it should not be seen in purely monetary terms. Often the key question is whether the available resources could be used differently to achieve the same goals and objectives. If less resources are used to achieve these goals, then there are savings in the use of resources. If the same level of resources is used to yield greater benefits, then there are gains in achievement. In both cases there is an increase in efficiency in the educational process. The resources in question include time and opportunity, as well as the usual human, physical and material resources in schools. When learners take seven years to complete a five-year course there is wastage which amounts to inefficiency. When teachers spend a good part of teaching time copying notes from a textbook on to the blackboard, for students to copy into their exercise books, this is a waste of time and opportunity which results in inefficiency.

Pedagogy in Practice

Learning is essentially about acquiring tools for living in the broadest possible sense. It is not simply about passing examinations, or taking in an undifferentiated deluge of information, or even acquiring a set of marketable skills. In the educational context, learning implies knowledge and this is much more than mere information. This is why we are normally critical of what is known as 'rote learning' or memorisation without understanding. The process of education entails promoting learning as the key with which individuals can have access to the extensive range of tools for living accumulated over the centuries and now enshrined in the various forms of human knowledge or disciplines available to us. The main challenge for good pedagogy is how to promote relevant, effective and efficient learning in the face of an ever-expanding range of human knowledge. Technology certainly has a major role to play in facilitating good pedagogy that can rise to this challenge.

Another important challenge for good pedagogy is how to ensure that learners can relate the achievements of schooling to the real world in which they live and function. One of the great mental tricks in playing the 'knowledge game' is to break up reality into various disciplines which then take on a life of their own as tools for exploring and creating knowledge as well as ways of understanding and mastering our world. This trick has enabled us over many centuries to become very effective and efficient in the business of learning as well as in making new knowledge and reshaping our world. On the one hand good pedagogy needs to exploit the rigour and depth of the various disciplines to promote effective and efficient learning. On the other hand, it is important that learners develop the ability to draw on and integrate aspects of these disciplines, in order to create a more holistic tool for understanding and acting on reality at different times and for different purposes. This is often facilitated by the creation of inter-disciplinary subject areas and integrated project work for learners.

Against the background of these and similar challenges, various categories of teaching styles have been used over the years to promote learning in the conventional education system. Technology can play a major role in improving pedagogy within all of these categories, but we need to make sound choices about what is best in different circumstances. In conventional schools, teaching styles are premised on assumptions of a cohort of more or less homogenous learners (similar age and ability) in the same grade, and progressing at the same pace through the system. Normally, this grouping of learners is dealt with on the basis of one teacher in charge for a given period of time, during which the business of teaching and learning takes place. There are usually several such encounters with different teachers in the course of a school day, and these periods of teaching and learning have come to represent what we regard as the rhythm of schooling. What teachers do individually and collectively during these periods is what defines the predominant teaching style in a school. In broad terms it is possible to categorise teaching styles as either teacher-centred or learner-centred. In practice, most teaching styles involve some combination of both approaches. The different styles of teaching are summarised in Table 4.1.

Table 4.1 Teaching Styles and the Use of Technology

Teaching style	Main pedagogical characteristics and implications for the use of technology
Teacher-centred approach	Focus is on the teacher as the source of knowledge. Teacher tends to be active while learners are expected to receive the knowledge being dispensed rather passively. The teacher talks; the learners listen. The teacher acts; the learners watch. Convenient for large class sizes. *Wide range of technologies can be used to aid the teacher's presentation and performance. Handouts, overhead projector (OHP) slides, models, etc. can all be used to capture and retain the learners' attention.*
Learner-centred approach	Emphasis is on learner as knowledge-seeker, with teacher as facilitator and guide. Learners tend to be active. They talk and do things in the process of learning. Teachers design and manage the setting as well as the process for learning. Difficult with large class sizes. *Technology can be used extensively to help learners make sense of the tasks assigned and learn what is required. However, there is usually a need for multiple units of the technology which all the learners need to use. Work sheets, models, equipment, etc., all need to be available to learners on an individual basis or in small groups.*
Combination of the two approaches	Attempts to strike a balance between the teacher as the main source of knowledge, and the learner as an active seeker of knowledge. In some matters the teacher dispenses knowledge and the learner has to take things on trust. At other times the teacher simply creates the conditions for the learner to explore and discover knowledge. At its best is highly interactive, with the focus shifting alternately from teacher to learners at different points in a lesson. *Technology can be used to aid the teacher's presentation as well as to assist learners in their exploration.*

Technology as an Aid to Teaching and Learning

The technology that can best serve as an aid to teaching and learning depends very much on the context. The latest or most sophisticated technology is not necessarily the most appropriate, even if it can be afforded. New technologies tend to have new requirements that determine their use – training, infrastructure and maintenance, for example. Using a new technology often implies much more than simply purchasing the technology.

Most old technologies, however, have a value and importance that is basic and fundamental to good pedagogy. We need to be careful about trivialising a technology simply because it has been around for a long time. It is instructive to consider the pedagogical uses of a random selection of technologies:

· *Chalk and board*: This technology has been unfairly caricatured in the literature. It is most closely associated with the so-called chalk-and-talk method of teaching, which has been heavily criticised due to its excessive use in poorer schools, and the tendency for untrained teachers to seek refuge in it as a safe pedagogy. In schools with very few resources it is not uncommon for untrained teachers to spend most of the teaching period copying notes from a textbook on to the board, for students to copy into their exercise books. This is the worst case scenario of wasted time and opportunity. However, the chalk and board technology can also be used in positive ways to improve the quality of teaching and learning. The mathematical problem set out on the board and solved step by step, with full participation of the whole class, can be a very rewarding learning experience. Similarly, the practice of getting learners to come up to the board and demonstrate something or write down an answer can be rewarding. Generally the chalk and board is used to note down key points as teacher and learners interact in the process of exploring a particular topic. Even when it is used to write down things for learners to copy, this can be a worthwhile exercise for young learners who need to develop the skills of 'copying from the board'. Some advantages of this technology are that it is long-lasting, requires little or no maintenance, and can be readily used with little training. It is cheap and uses chalk, which is an easily obtained resource. Small boards can be provided for young learners to use, especially when they are learning to write or need to practice a lot, but cannot afford to waste other resources like paper and pencil.

· *Overhead projector (OHP)*: In one sense this technology is akin to a modern electronic chalk and board, but it is much more versatile. As with chalk and board, it enables the teacher to 'write and display' to the learners in real time. However, it also enables the teacher to display material prepared in advance. It is very versatile in terms of what can be displayed, ranging from notes and diagrams prepared by the teacher, to complex diagrams and photographs copied electronically on to the OHP transparency. Another advantage is that the same transparencies can be preserved and re-used as a teaching resource. The OHP allows the teacher to make use of an extensive range of illustrations and notes that are readily available. So the teacher can focus on the interactive business of teaching and learning, instead of spending time and effort writing and drawing on the board. On the downside, the OHP requires electricity supply and regular maintenance as well as a supply of special transparency sheets and special pens. These cost factors have to be weighed against the advantages of the OHP as a pedagogical tool.

- *Charts, maps, photographs, handouts, etc.*: These technologies have the main advantage of enabling the teacher to present 'ready-made' illustrations and aids, rather than do these in real time that should be devoted to the interactive process of learning and teaching. As pedagogical tools they promote more effective and efficient learning, in line with the notion that 'a picture speaks a thousand words'. These are technologies that lend themselves to all situations. Every teacher can prepare them in some form and make use of them in the classroom. They can also be mass produced in standard versions and supplied to schools.

- *Textbooks*: This is by far the most widely used technology in efforts to improve the quality of teaching and learning. Its importance and effectiveness have been emphasised by several studies showing that 'textbook availability' is the single most important variable that influences the quality of primary education in many developing countries. The best textbooks serve both as a guide to good teaching and an aid to self-learning. In terms of unit cost, textbooks must rank among the lowest-cost technologies, yet availability of textbooks continues to be a major issue and problem in most developing countries. This is a complex matter having to do with the publishing industry that deals with the development and production of textbooks. Many countries still lack a strong publishing industry and the business of developing and producing textbooks can be very expensive under in such conditions. Talk of one day getting computers and relevant software into every school should be treated with great caution in a world that has so far failed to get a simple textbook into the hands of every child in every classroom.

- *Programmed learning materials*: These technologies include workbooks that accompany some textbooks; self-learning texts as used in distance education, and the interactive electronic gadgets used for self-paced learning exercises. The main advantage of these technologies is that they help to promote learning with minimal involvement of a teacher. They also make it possible for learning to be centred on the level of ability and progress of the individual learner, rather than on some class average. Unfortunately, formal schools tend not to benefit fully from the advantages offered by these technologies, because they are used more in non-formal and distance-learning programmes than in regular schools.

- *Radio and audio recorders*: These technologies enable the teacher to bring other resource persons into the classroom through their voices. They can also be used for illustrative purposes, such as getting learners to hear musical scores or listen to forest noises. The use of recorders in particular enables the teacher to prepare good quality audio-learning aids that can then be used over and over again in the classroom whenever required. These technologies require electrical power, but even where the infrastructure is not available it is possible to use batteries and even human muscle power (wind-up radio). The issue of cost is still a problem for many countries, although unit costs of radios and audio recorders have decreased steadily over the years.

- *Television and video recorders*: These technologies represent the interactive and dynamic versions of charts, pictures, slides, etc. They also enable the teacher to bring other resource persons into the classroom through their images as well as their voices. Like the radio and audio recorder, they can be used for a wide variety of illustration, and they have the added advantage of engaging the eyes as well as the ears of learners.

· *Computers*: This currently ranks as the ultimate technology available for teaching and learning, especially when it is linked into the world-wide web. The potential versatility of this technology is enormous, and in time it could subsume most of the functions and advantages of other educational technologies. Computers offer teachers great possibilities in terms of the range of materials they can prepare for use in their classrooms, through word processing, spread sheets, graphics, etc. They can also be used to teach these very skills to learners as part of preparing them for the modern world where they are increasingly a part of life in the work-place. In the classroom, computers can be used in conjunction with special projectors to perform functions similar to the OHP and the slide projector. The best functions of programmed learning can be performed with the computer. Software packages exist for self-instruction in a wide range of areas. The computer is the tool *par excellence* for self-learning. Most importantly the computer can be used to access the world-wide web, where both teachers and learners can discover an infinite range of materials and pedagogical aids. The case study on Mathematics teaching (page 115) shows that there is much that teachers and learners can get directly from the web on various topics.

Overview of Current Practices

It is encouraging that most countries appreciate and value the key role of teachers, and focus on their training and professional development as a critical factor in policies and strategies for improving quality in education. However, we are still a long way from developing the combination of policies and strategies that will be best suited to preparing the most appropriate teachers for our schools in an era of globalisation. It is not clear that serious efforts are being made to build key technology elements into teacher training courses. In many countries there have been no major revisions to courses dealing with the use of technology for pedagogy and improvements in the quality of education. Indeed, in most countries, such changes as have been made in teacher training have been due to expediency in dealing with course restraints, rather than to sound pedagogical considerations.

The old model of preparing teachers through several years pre-service education and some practice teaching, or short period of pupillage, has proved to be very resilient in most countries. Where this has changed, invariably it has been due to constraints on time and cost, rather than for pedagogical reasons. For instance, when a country declares universal primary education over night, or decides to expand enrolment rapidly, there is a need to have trained teachers in place at a faster rate than can be delivered through the usual two- or three-year pre-service training programmes. Moreover, such a country may not be in a position to afford the short-term costs of rapidly expanding student enrolment at its teacher training colleges, necessary to produce the required numbers of trained teachers. In such situations, innovative 'crash training' programmes tend to come into being. Although these are often hailed as a significant breakthrough in teacher training strategies, they are seldom regarded as being on a par with conventional pre-service training. At best they enable countries to cope with the constraints involved in getting adequate numbers of trained teachers into the system. What is positive about these innovations is that they have helped to focus attention on issues of content and entry requirements for teacher training programmes, the duration of these programmes and how they should be structured over time to provide the most effective and efficient teacher training strategy for a country.

Unfortunately much of the current debate in most countries has tended to neglect the pedagogical considerations relating to content and duration. The focus has been on a search for 'quick fix' answers to questions of how to train more teachers, more cost effectively (code for cheaply), and in a much shorter time. This focus has seen a shift towards shorter pre-service education, less demanding intake requirements and more emphasis on training while teaching. The process has been facilitated by the use of distance education for teacher training, which helps to explain a current trend towards emphasising the advantages of using distance education in this way. While most of the advantages claimed in this regard cannot be disputed, it would be most unfortunate if the essential point of distance education came to be seen as training more teachers cheaply. The use of distance education in teacher training assumes that what should be the focus of such training is not the most problematic issue, and that there are no serious difficulties with how the training provided should be used. It is only when we begin to address these matters that current practice will begin to shift towards a more sensible basis for selecting and using appropriate technologies for improving pedagogy.

In this regard, it needs to be acknowledged that efforts are being made in many countries to shift from the old teacher-centred pedagogy to a more learner-centred approach. A wide range of in-service programmes are designed to train teachers in child-centred methodology and make them aware of the kinds of changes they need to introduce in the classroom. However, attendance at such training programmes is not a guarantee of change in the classroom. The persistence of large class sizes makes it difficult for teachers to put child-centred techniques into practice, and the shortage of teaching/learning technologies in most schools leaves teachers with very little choice other than to teach in a didactic manner. How does a teacher with a class of 80 or more pupils and no technology aid promote discovery learning, or help different children to learn at their own pace? These pedagogical considerations must also be addressed. The methods and techniques used in multi-grade teaching may well prove relevant in large classes in which there is a need for greater emphasis on self-paced learning, small-group work and the discovery approach. It will also be necessary to have a reasonable complement of technology that would make multi-grade techniques feasible. In general, it may be time to shift from the economics of course content, structure, duration and intake qualification for teacher training, towards the pedagogy of how to help real teachers bring about real change in real classrooms!

Addressing the Challenges

Learning how to learn is ultimately the greatest challenge facing education in the age of globalisation. There continues to be an exponential increase in the volume and complexity of what we need to learn in order to function in the modern world. However, human beings are naturally equipped to cope with this rapid expansion in knowledge and information through their innate mental ability to select, structure and organise information and knowledge in multifarious ways, to deal with every specific situation. Human beings have been very successful at augmenting, extending and improving this natural ability to cope with information and knowledge.

We have long used technology to reinforce and boost our capacity to make abstract and symbolic representations of our world, as well as our ability to process rapidly and manipulate the resulting concepts, principles and rules in infinite ways. We have therefore been able to use technology to create new realities and new tools, not only for understanding our world but also for acting on it and re-creating it in new ways. All these possibilities are potentially available to anyone who has mastered the business of learning how to learn. It is clear that technology can help to facilitate this process.

Given the continuing expansion in knowledge and information, and the proliferation of possible sources, the process of education can no longer be confined to mastering a finite selection of prescribed content. Increasingly it has to be about mastering the business of learning how to learn, which is the passport to the wealth of information and knowledge available in the modern world. It also has to be about what is most relevant to learners, rather than what is prescribed by others. How can we bring about the major shift in focus and the change in pedagogy and curriculum that are necessary to achieve this mastery of learning how to learn what we need to learn? In what ways can technology play a role in this area that is so important for quality education?

Training teachers and providing for their continued professional development is the second most important challenge facing education systems in most Commonwealth countries. For many of these countries the task is nothing short of rediscovering the professionalism that should characterise teaching. In this regard the most important point to be acknowledged is that pedagogical expertise, rather than knowledge of an academic discipline, is at the heart of teaching as a profession. A good teacher is not one who knows everything in a discipline, but one who knows *where* to find things about a discipline; *how* to find out things in a discipline, and *what* to do with what one finds. This is what good pedagogy is really about. It is what sets teachers apart from others who may also promote learning in various settings outside school systems.

The next important point to acknowledge is that developing an appropriate range of good pedagogical skills is more a matter of long-term experiential learning than short-term conceptual learning. This raises important questions about the length and emphasis of college-based teacher education courses. It also highlights the need for more attention to be given to in-service training and on-going support for the professional self-development of teachers. The challenge is for teachers to become more reflective about their own practice and to take greater responsibility for their professional self-development.

A third important challenge is to facilitate the role of people other than teachers in the business of using appropriate pedagogy for improving the quality of education. Good teachers have always recognised the importance of using other resource persons in the process of promoting learning. Taking learners for a museum visit; using local elders to teach about village history; making use of craftspeople to teach practical skills, are all examples of how teachers use others to improve the quality of education. This kind of pedagogy will become increasingly important, given the explosion in modern knowledge and information, and the wide diversity of sources and expertise that now exists outside the school and is potentially available to learners.

Improving the tools for good pedagogy and making them more widely available to teachers and learners is another important challenge that needs to be addressed. In the case of teachers, it highlights the need for greater interaction and peer support that will enhance professional skills-development. Teachers need to share good practice more among themselves, and encourage collaborative efforts to improve pedagogy. The future of teaching hinges on professional self-development by individuals and professional self-reinforcement by the profession as a whole.

Formulating Policies and Strategies

The remaking of the teaching profession should be at the heart of policies concerned with pedagogy and improved quality in education. The main goal of such policies should be to help create a teaching force that is:

- focused on mastering the business of planning and managing the settings and the processes through which learning takes place;
- concerned with promoting and strengthening active self-learning, rather than with passive acquisition of knowledge and information;
- geared to promoting and supporting professional self-development efforts on a systematic and sustained basis;
- committed to the appropriate use of technology as an aid to teaching and learning;
- dedicated to reflecting on their own practice and seeking constant improvements; and
- willing to try out a range of technologies that may be relevant to improving the learning process.

Strategies for introducing technology that relates to good pedagogy and improvements in the quality of education should focus on teachers. Ultimately they hold the key to what happens in classrooms and they must be at the centre of technological change. Against this background the following factors must be taken into account:

- teachers need access to centres where they can safely try out various types of technologies and seek help where necessary;
- schools need leadership that is committed to using technology for pedagogical purposes, and that is supportive of teachers in this regard;
- strategies should focus on introducing technologies that are affordable and can be maintained within reasonable budgets; and
- a comprehensive approach should be taken in selecting technologies, so that they can serve multiple purposes in the education system (pedagogy, management, access, etc.).

Decisions on policies and strategies for technology to improve pedagogy will not be based on pedagogical considerations alone. Issues of cost and affordability are likely to be major factors that will influence any conclusions and recommendations to decision-makers in each country. Indeed, much detailed work needs to be done to give a full cost-benefit analysis of proposed technologies before a decision is taken. In this regard consideration should be given not only to the fixed costs of setting up and making the technology functional (buying the equipment, constructing infrastructure, designing software, preparing print and audio-visual materials, etc.); but also to the variable costs that will increase according to the number of users (teachers' time, print runs, end-user supplies, etc.), and to other recurrent costs that must be regularly budgeted for over time, such as maintenance, electricity, telephone and other utilities and service charges associated with the technology.

As a rule, the less technology there is in conventional schools the lower the fixed costs will be, and the more technology there is the higher the fixed costs will be. It is important to appreciate that introducing new technologies into a school system bring in higher fixed costs which make education more expensive. Such additional costs need to be justified in terms of the pedagogical and quality gains likely to result from the introduction of these new technologies. However, most modern technologies also yield economies of scale that often more than make up for their high fixed costs. For instance, good programmed learning material involves high fixed costs in terms of initial development, but it can be reproduced for a whole education system at relatively little additional cost. The high fixed costs can therefore be spread over the large number of copies, thereby providing economies of scale. This makes each copy of the material relatively inexpensive and therefore justifiable in terms of the purchase cost.

Another general rule is that low technology in a school system usually implies high variable costs, particularly in terms of teachers' time. If teachers do everything with little or no technology, more teachers are required. They must spend more time on preparation and have more contact time in order to achieve a similar pedagogical impact to a system with reasonable technological aid. Indeed, a common justification for the introduction of technology in education systems is that it will produce savings in terms of teachers' costs, while improving the quality of the learning process in schools.

All these and similar cost considerations can make decision-making a very complex process. It is therefore useful to explore cost issues in a more aggregated manner, in terms of standard indicators such as unit learner cost, or the cost of producing each graduate from a training programme. These indicators can be used as part of a model to explore how costs change with the introduction of different kinds of technology into the system, or even into each kind of institution.

Case Study 4: The Training Implications of the ICT Revolution on Secondary Mathematics

Douglas Butler

Director, Centre for ICT Training and Research,
Oundle School, Oundle, UK

New Opportunities and Challenges for the Secondary Mathematics Teacher

Mathematics is possibly unique among school subjects: not only is it taught the world over, but school children in nearly every country learn much the same content. The language of delivery varies, of course, but the written notation (certainly in 'western' cultures) is mostly the same, and the opportunities presented by ICT are there to be shared by all.

Since the subject came into being, the dedicated enthusiasm of countless generations of teachers has educated the worlds' school children in the finer points of Mathematics using no more than a piece of chalk – and this is how it still is in the majority of Mathematics classrooms today.

A growing number of Mathematics teachers are now beginning to discover what the ICT revolution has to offer, not only in their own personal productivity, but as a teaching aid in the classroom (Figure 4.1). This study aims to summarise some of the variety and sparkle that can be added to a lesson if the teacher is trained and has access to appropriate software and hardware. The corresponding visualisation of the subject can dramatically improve pupils' motivation – in particular it can open the eyes of the more reluctant pupils who regard Mathematics as a dreaded necessity!

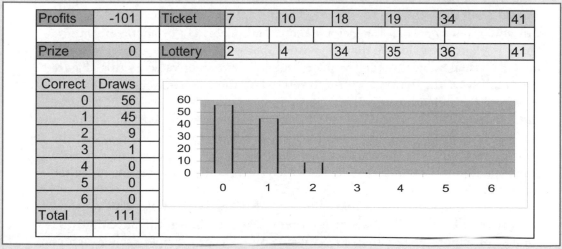

Profits	-101		Ticket	7	10	18	19	34	41
Prize	0		Lottery	2	4	34	35	36	41
Correct	Draws								
0	56								
1	45								
2	9								
3	1								
4	0								
5	0								
6	0								
Total	111								

Figure 4.1 A Spreadsheet Simulation of a Series of National Lottery Draws, Indicating How Often Correct Matches were Obtained, and the Net Loss After a Number of Draws, Used to Illustrate the Underlying Principles of Probability and Chance (DISCUS Project, University of Coventry, UK)

The Challenge

It is a major concern that the world's schools are becoming more and more polarised between those that have plenty of access to ICT, and those that have none. It is also the intention of this study to explore what can be achieved in ICT using modest resources, and to try to prioritise spending when budgets are tight (Appendix 1, page 123).

Teachers fortunate enough to have new ICT resources to hand are now faced with an embarrassment of riches. The challenge is to train teachers to select them carefully, and above all to use new methods sparingly. Many observers of computer-enabled classes are surprised at how little, but how effectively, the new methods are employed – the majority of a lesson is still undertaken by traditional means.   The ICT opportunity is easily wasted if misused or over-used.

The Impact and Scope of New Software in the Secondary Mathematics Curriculum

Perhaps more than any other school subject, Mathematics has a rich source of new methods to draw on using ICT. It is convenient to group these as follows, though inevitably there will be more and more overlap as the products evolve:

- *The graph plotter – e.g. Autograph, Omnigraph, Coypu:* This is probably the most important software group: the graph plotter has great scope for visualising many of the basic concepts in Mathematics. Also, this group is not expensive, and there are some very adequate plotters available for free down-load from the internet.
- *The spreadsheet – e.g. Excel:* This important tool, designed for the business community, is now firmly established as a mathematical tool for schools. The ability to perform repetitive calculations and create graphs from data can give great satisfaction to pupils.
- *Statistical analysis – e.g. DataDesk, Fathom, Minitab, Discus:* With the increasing occurrence of statistics in the world's school Mathematics curricula, teachers can bring in 'real life' data from the internet and enliven their classes with computer-assisted analysis.
- *Dynamic geometry – e.g. Geometer's Sketchpad, Cabri II, Geometry Inventor:* There is plenty of evidence that this visual approach to the teaching of a fundamentally visual subject is very popular, and pupils are motivated by this (Figure 4.2). However, the dynamic approach offered by the computer can very rarely substitute for a rigorous pencil-and-paper proof.
- *Mathematical DTP – e.g. Word (MS Equation Editor), MathCad:* The simple way to type Mathematics is to use a combination of superscript (for indices) and the standard symbols font (for various mathematical signs). For more complex expressions, the Equation Editor that comes with Word is effective, creating an editable graphic of the formula.
- *CDs – e.g. Escher, Art and Mathematics, MathWise, TransMath:* This medium may prove to be short-lived as the internet takes over, but in the meantime a number of important resources are available on CD, for example Escher pictures and a growing number of CDs for revision, or for structured learning (known as 'interactive learning systems').

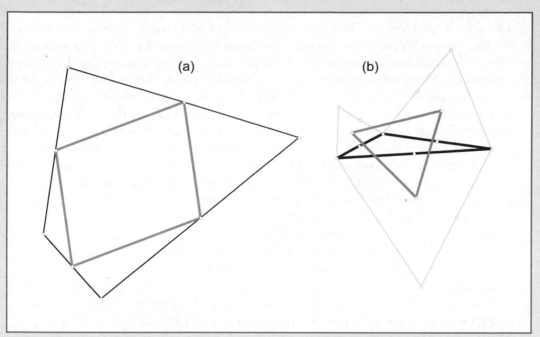

Figure 4.2 Two Examples of Dynamic Geometry: (a) Illustrates the Theorem that the Mid Points of the Sides of Any Quadrilateral Form a Parallelogram; (b) Illustrates Napoleon's Theorem (Geometer's Sketchpad)

- *Symbolic algebra systems – e.g. Derive, MathView:* What is becoming clear from this category is that algebraic software can now do much of the Mathematics that is taught in schools (Figure 4.3). The challenge therefore is increasingly not only how to teach the subject, but what to teach.

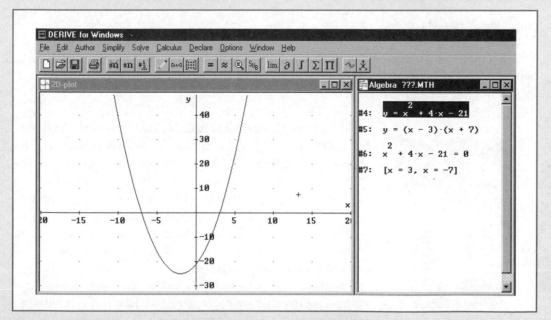

Figure 4.3 The Use of an Algebra Window Alongside a Plotting Window Allows a Symbolic Algebra Package to be Used to Illustrate a Number of Properties of the Standard Factorisable Quadratic (Screen Created Using Derive)

- *Hand-held calculators*: These are getting cheaper and more powerful almost daily. So far, solar-powered calculators are restricted to the small screen 'scientific' category. Graphic models can handle numerical, graphing, algebraic and statistical operations. Many calculators can connect to OHP pallets for class display. The disadvantages are the low resolution images and awkward keyboard entry.
- *The internet, e-mail and video conferencing*: This category is the most significant development so far and warrants a study in its own right. Mathematics is a global subject and there is already a huge bank of resources available to teachers from all over the world. Teachers need to learn how to find them, and how to incorporate data and graphics into their worksheets, and in their day-to-day teaching. (For an example of a worksheet based on internet resources, see Appendix 2, page 124). Oundle School has made a good starting resource available on: http://www.argonet.co.uk/oundlesch/.

  Email has a special potential, as teachers can use specialist discussion lists to contact other teachers and professional organisations.

  The ability to send and receive pictures and sound over the internet is now a reality. The PC camera is cheap (or you can use a regular video camera); the communications software is very versatile and is free (Net-Meeting from Microsoft). This allows both parties to share a white board, chat line and any applications that one or other is running (e.g. a spreadsheet). We can now look forward to the prospect of affordable distance teaching.

Appendix 3 (page 125) lists school-level Mathematics topics suitable for ICT treatment.

The Impact and Scope of New Hardware on the Learning Environment in Secondary Mathematics

Whole-Class Teaching

Whole-class instruction can now benefit from a dynamic new teaching environment using computer-generated images. To achieve an image that is large enough to be seen by the pupils, the options are:

Figure 4.4 Whole-Class Instruction Can Benefit From the Use of Computer-Generated Images

- *a large television (with a suitable adaptor)* – the image is a bit grainy, but this is the most affordable solution, and has the surprising benefit of being able to write on the television screen with an ordinary white-board marker.
- *a 'Cruiser' laptop* – this is a new concept: a high performance PC laptop with a detachable screen that then acts as an OHP pallet. The image is bright enough for most conditions, and a remote keyboard and mouse can be passed around the class for pupil input.
- *a computer projector* – ideal, but at the time of writing still prohibitively expensive for schools. Ideally it should be ceiling-mounted, shining on to a white writing surface. This avoids the glare that follows from projecting horizontally, and the teacher can also write on the image.

Using the ICT Laboratory

With a classroom display system, the teacher remains in control, driving the pace. Taking a class to a lab needs careful thought, and the essential ingredient is the well-planned worksheet to ensure that the pupils benefit from a worthwhile learning experience. Pupil-controlled images add interest and there is scope for working with peers (Figure 4.5).

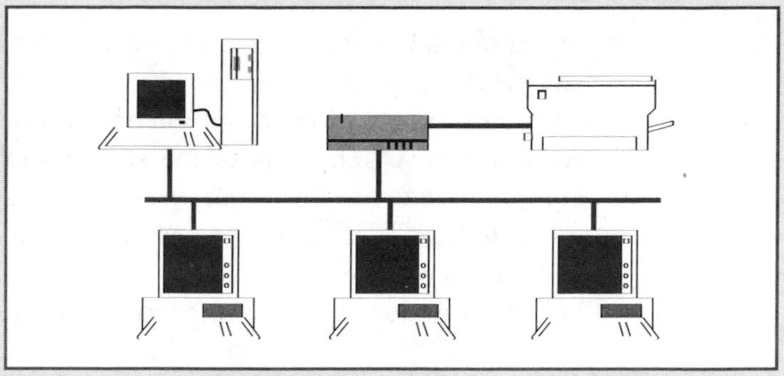

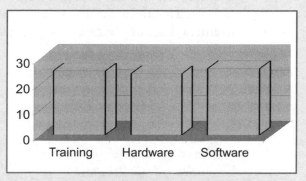

Figure 4.5 Using an ICT Laboratory Gives Scope for Pupils to Work with their Peers

Training Strategies for a Secondary Mathematics Department

The first objectives are:

- *To plan for equal provision of the three essential ingredients*: training, hardware and software (Figure 4.6). Lagging behind with any one will lead to opportunities in the other two being wasted: for example, trained teachers with no ICT support, or brand new equipment being ignored by teachers unaware of the possibilities. The most common error is to assume that funds are needed only for hardware and that somehow the other two will just happen!

Figure 4.6 The Equal Provision of Training, Hardware and Software is Essential

- *To convince school and curriculum managers that Mathematics is a subject that can materially benefit from investment in ICT.* Despite the many opportunities that will be obvious to the committed user, this objective can be difficult to achieve in the light of many centuries of successful teaching without them. Also without the informed backing of school heads and their deputies, an ICT departmental programme is likely to founder.

Face-to-Face Training

Within each academic department a member of staff needs to be asked to act as an ICT 'anchor'. This person will provide the leadership necessary to see a training programme launched and followed through in the department.

The 'anchor' should attend a regional training day, which would aim to cover an introduction to the general and subject-specific skills. The format should be part presentation (when the trainer dictates the pace) and part hands-on workshop, with no more than 16 in the group. The departmental 'anchor' should have the confidence to start using ICT methods to improve personal productivity (word-processing and spreadsheets) and consider the following objectives:

- review existing hardware and software provision in the department;
- review existing ICT expertise within the department;

- recommend hardware and software purchases, probably a rolling programme over two to three years;
- advise on integration of a departmental network with the school's network plans;
- recommend which parts of the syllabus can benefit from ICT methods;
- compose a two to three-year training schedule for the rest of the department;
- indicate how ICT can increase personal productivity using word-processing and spreadsheets; and
- lay the foundations for a departmental intranet for electronic storage of resources.

This is a significant challenge even for an ICT-literate teacher.

On-Line Training

Those schools fortunate enough to be able to send an 'anchor' teacher to a regional training day will have made a good start, but training must be ongoing, and there is also the need to train the other members of the department. There can never be enough trainers for this 'face-to-face' approach, and the internet offers a very practicable solution, requiring:

- teachers who are motivated to learn this way;
- reasonably fast internet connectivity;
- training materials of sufficient quality, and in the local language; and
- on-line tutorial help.

Face-to-face and on-line training can be combined (Figure 4.7).

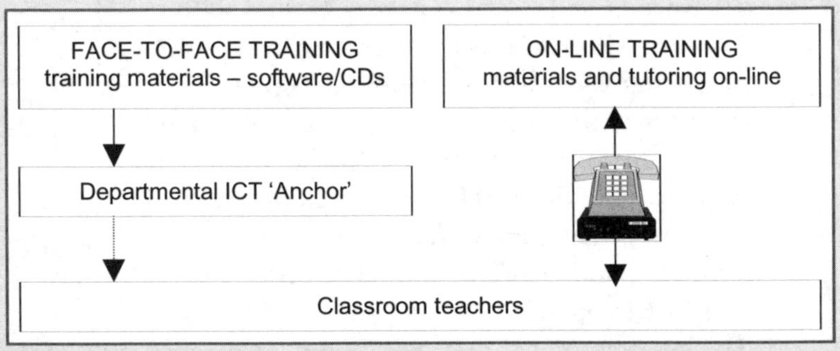

Figure 4.7 Face-to-Face and On-Line Training can be Combined to Train Classroom Teachers

Teacher Ownership of Hardware

It is important that any training programme devised for Mathematics teachers includes the use of ICT to help with their personal productivity. This should include word-processing for work-sheets, using e-mail as a professional communications tool, and using the internet as a classroom resource. Experience has shown that confidence with this technology cannot be really secure until a teacher owns a computer or has easy access to one at school and at home.

It should be a high priority in any ICT master plan, to assist with a teacher purchase scheme (if there is a likelihood of the teachers being able to afford one). It is also likely that portable computers will get cheaper and more powerful.

Already mentioned is the 'Cruiser' laptop with detachable lid for whole-class teaching. If a school authority is encouraging teachers to own their own machines, this solution is attractive because it provides the classroom computer and display system all at once. The solution is also particularly appropriate for schools that do not have class-rooms dedicated to Mathematics.

The Cost Implications of Technology in the Curriculum

This is undoubtedly the most difficult area of this subject, with all three cost centres – training, software and hardware – greatly affected by local variations.

Face-to-Face Training

When any country starts to add up the number of hours of training required to bring even one teacher per school up to speed with the use of ICT in the classroom, the figures immediately suggest a major investment in time and resources. One full day per 'anchor' teacher and at least two half-day follow-ups are recommended. The cost of training and supporting the trainers is also significant, especially as they are likely to be seconded from the classroom.

On-Line Training

On-line training needs to be set up by local governments, tailored to local needs, including language. On-line tutors need to be trained and in place.

Purchase of Software

There is an increasing availability of high quality software free of charge from the internet. The list includes graph plotters, a dynamic geometry package and a large number of 'Java' internet applications that can be down-loaded legally. These are obviously not as polished as the commercial applications, but represent a good start for a cash-starved Mathematics department.

Of the commercial products, a graph plotter, a word-processor, a spreadsheet and possibly a dynamic geometry package should be the first items to go for. The unit cost can be reduced considerably by buying site licences.

Purchase of Hardware

With so many schools in the world struggling to find basic resources it will be useful to consider first what you can achieve with the bare minimum, and progress from there:

- *No electricity*
  - wind-up technology is here, and able to power simple computers;
  - solar-powered devices are not yet powerful enough to perform more than simple calculations;
  - mobile power units that generate electricity for small networks have been trialled.
- *No telephone connection*
  the only feasible way to connect to the internet without a land-line is through a satellite connection. With the internet having such enormous potential in remote areas, it is likely that this method of connectivity will be a priority for the local educational technology planners.
- *Just old computers and no funds to upgrade*
  there is a surprising amount that Mathematics teachers can achieve with old equipment (say 286- and 386-DOS computers). A number of important mathematical products were sufficiently well developed before the advent of Windows that their early DOS versions are still useful and still available. In particular Excel (spreadsheet), Derive (symbolic algebra) and Cabri Geometre (dynamic geometry).

• *With a school network in place*
the network is the backbone of ICT success. With it resources and applications can be shared around the community. Another significant development is a networking tool that will allow older computers to sit on a modern network and act as 'dumb terminals' (or 'thin clients'). The picture is only just becoming clear, but the implications for under-resourced schools are obvious: the hardware that sits on the end of a network is likely to get cheaper and cheaper.

A useful site giving direct links to software and hardware suppliers can be found at: http://www.argonet.co.uk/oundlesch/suppl.html. It is divided into categories as follows:

• general suppliers (UK)
• symbolic algebra
• geometry packages
• graph plotters
• spreadsheets and statistics packages
• interactive learning systems (ILS)
• mathematical DTP
• graphic calculators
• advisory.

Conclusions

The main concern with ICT in schools is that there is a serious likelihood of scarce resources being wasted on software and hardware that is inappropriately used or not used at all. Everyone is clamouring for computers and far too many are being installed in schools throughout the world without due thought for their use.

The hardware that delivers the software is certain to change, and become more and more affordable, especially when connected to a network. It is also likely that the comparatively inexpensive calculators and palm-top categories will gradually close the performance gap to provide rich learning tools for pupils to use in the classroom.

Mathematics is fortunate – there are many obvious advantages to using ICT methods in the teaching and learning process, and this is not the case in many school subjects. Yet however obvious the advantages, training teachers to put them into practice is vital.

Clearly what is now needed is an international initiative to set up a programme for training the trainers, and at the same time a parallel initiative to put these training resources on the internet so they can be made available to all.

Some useful world-wide web sites for teaching Mathematics are listed in Appendix 4 (page 126).

Appendices

Appendix 1: ICT Basic Skills for Teaching and Learning Mathematics

The ICT revolution is advancing to affect nearly all aspects of human activity, and the evolution of the internet has accelerated this process. Education is not exempt, and teachers and students the world over are being offered exciting new challenges.

Both teachers and students need to discover and practise a range of ICT-related skills. Table 4.2 is a 'starter list'. Curriculum planners must consider carefully how to make available the time for teachers to be trained, and which subjects are to give the time for students to be trained.

Table 4.2 A Starter List of ICT Skills for Teachers and Students

General skills

Hardware
basic connections: monitor, printer, keyboard, mouse; installing new software; running software; loading, saving, deleting files; copying images from any package; connecting to a projector; manipulating bit-map images

Spreadsheet
cell co-ordinates; entering text; entering data; entering a formula; split screen working; relative and absolute cell references; fill-down; selecting one or more (non-adjacent) columns; drawing a scatter diagram; importing data from an internet page; incorporating an Excel sheet within Word; using spreadsheets for record keeping (marks, orders, grading, etc)

Graph plotting
entering an equation; setting the scales; zooming; drawing a tangent, normal; reading co-ordinates; plotting families; cartesian, parametric and polar co-ordinates

Sketchpad
drawing points and lines; multiple selections; simple constructions; simple use of scripts; deleting and hiding objects

Word processing
typing and simple formatting of text; copying and pasting images; using the symbols font for simple Mathematics; using the equation editor (in Word); importing text and graphics from the internet

Algebra
using a symbolic manipulator (eg Derive); input notation; factor, expand, solve; calculus: differentiation, integration; plotting functions

Scientific calculator and graphic calculator
routine calculations; trigonometry calculations (radians/degrees); graphical work (axes scales); data input and statistical calculations

Internet skills

World-wide web
connecting to a modem or to the network; loading a browser; browsing off-line; entering a URL; copying a URL; using the favourites list; moving between visited pages; the use of page-up and page-down; selecting text and graphics to copy and paste; sensible use of search engines; downloading software, and 'plug-ins'; learning to authenticate a web site

Email
sending and receiving messages; subscribing to email discussion groups; managing attachments; copying text from an email; launching a URL from within an email

Video conferencing
Microsoft NetMeeting: using the whiteboard, chat, sound and video

HTML worksheets
using Microsoft Word (Office 97) to incorporate live URLs and text/graphics from web pages.

Appendix 2: Using Internet Resources to Make a Work Sheet

Teachers can use the resources available on the internet and incorporate data and graphics into their worksheets. Figure 4.8 is an example.

You are to use the resources of the internet to investigate Pythagorean triples. The following headings are suggested:

1. The simplest Pythagorean triple is 3 - 4 - 5, since $3^2 + 4^2 = 5^2$. Before looking at any web sites, write down any more that you know about Pythagorean triples.

2. On the Autograph 'Lists' site of Pythagorean triples, what do you think the numbers in square brackets mean? How has this list been ordered?

3. Do you notice that for a number of triples the difference between the two largest sides is one?
Show that in this case the sides can be represented by $\acute{U}(2n+1)$, n and (n+1).
See if you can copy this Autograph list into a spreadsheet.

4. With reference to the Autograph 'Lists' site of prime numbers, note that the year 1997 was both 'pythagorean' and 'prime'. What year does this next happen? How would you show that 1997 is prime?

5. Look at the 25 proofs of Pythagoras' theorem and find one that you would like to record.

6. Who was Pythagoras? See if you can download his portrait from the biography site quoted below, and incorporate it in a poster of your findings.

Some suggested web sites to visit:

1. Autograph lists
http://www.acorn.com/developers/autograph/calc/lists.html
2. 25 proofs of Pythagoras' theorem
http://www.cut-the-knot.com/pythagoras/
3. Pythagoras of Samos
http://euler.ciens.ucv.ve/English/mathematics/pitagora.html

Figure 4.8 A Worksheet Based on Internet Resources

Appendix 3: Mathematical Topics Suitable for ICT Treatment

Table 4.3 shows some school-level Mathematics topics suitable for ICT treatment.

Table 4.3 School-Level Mathematics Topics Suitable for ICT Treatment

---

11–16 year-old Mathematics

Internet resources can be useful, e.g.:
Number: prime numbers, irrational numbers;
measures; time; money; Greenwich time site
World camera sites, (to study longitude)
Currency converter site
Statistics and data handling: data sources
A growing list of topics can be found on
Interactive Java sites (e.g. from Japan), including
proofs of Pythagoras' theorem; transformations

Spreadsheet methods can be used to investigate
various topics, e.g.:
Number: number sequences; nth term
Displaying data

A graph plotter can be used by the teacher and
pupils to explore relationships and illustrate basic
function concepts, e.g.:
f(x) and inverse, f'(x) · graphs in practical situations;
straight line graphs: gradient/intercept
$y = kx^n$ (n=-2, -1, 0, 1, 2, 3); tangents to curves;
investigating y = mx+c

Solutions of equations and inequalities
Solving linear and quadratic equations
Graphical representations of inequalities
Visualising transformations

Dynamic geometry packages offer new ways to
explore geometrical relationships, e.g.:
Constructions; bearings; symmetry
Angle (parallel lines, triangles, quadrilaterals,
polygons, circles); locus; mensuration; transformations

Statistics packages:
Histograms; cumulative frequency

Post-16 Mathematics

Here, the **graph plotter** can be particularly valuable as an aid to the visualisation of functional
analysis:
The general quadrativ
Implicit lines, circle and ellipse

Curves and equations, transformations
Parametric and polar co-ordinates
Six trigonometric ratios and identities
Circular measure and Trig formulae
Solution of trig equations
Sin, cos, tan for small angles
Functions; inverse, composition
Exponential and logarithmic functions
Differentiation, inverse trig, ax, lnx
Composite functions, turning points
Definite integrals; areas and volumes
Rational functions

Hyperbolic functions and inverses
Further differentiation and integration
Mean values, centroids, arc lengths, volumes
First and second order differential equations
Simple Harmonic Motion
Curve sketching, $y^2 = f(x)$, $y = |f(x)|$
Numerical solution of equations
Maclaurin's series
Numerical integration (e.g. trapezium rule)
Matrices and transformations

A spreadsheet can be used to study:
Sequences, APs, GPs
Solution of equations: bisection, x = g(x),
Newton-Raphson
Numerical integration (e.g. Simpson's rule)
Step-by-step methods for solving differential
equations
Curve fitting by least squares

Statistics packages:
Scatter diagrams; linear regression
Binomial , normal and poisson distributions
Sampling; confidence intervals

Appendix 4: Some Useful World-Wide Web Sites for Teaching Mathematics

A good reference site is http://www.argonet.co.uk/oundlesch/mlink.html, which divides the mathematical use of the internet as follows:

· Mathematical associations and magazines
· Mathematical resources
· Mathematical entertainment
· Statistical resources
· Other lists of useful links

For a fuller treatment, see *Using the Internet: Mathematics* by Douglas Butler, published by Pearson Publishing, Cambridge (March 1998).

A revolution is taking place in Mathematics teaching at secondary and college level, and TSM is pioneering an approach to teacher training that is both informative and practical. Teachers can discover ideas that add variety and a guaranteed sparkle to their lessons. Table 4.4 is an example of a TSM programme.

Table 4.4 A Typical TSM Programme

What's going on in other subjects eg Music (Sibelius – Music Processor)	**Mathematical DTP** Word (Microsoft, USA) MathType (Chartwell-Yorke)
Spreadsheets Excel-97 (Microsoft, USA)	**ILS (Integrated Learning Systems)** Transmath (Leeds University)
Graph plotters Autograph (Oundle School) Omnigraph (Sheringham High School) Coypu (Shell Centre, Nottingham)	**Statistics** Discus project (Coventry University) Autograph (Oundle School)
Geometry Cabri Géomètre-2 (Univ. Grenoble) Geometer's Sketchpad	**CDs** Escher Art and Mathematics
Symbolic algebra systems Derive (Soft Warehouse) MathCad (Waterloo Maple, USA)	**The internet, email and video conferencing** A rapidly growing resource

Notes

TSM is a teacher training activity based at Oundle School, Peterborough (UK), which tries to get to grips with the explosion of new products and ideas in this field. There have been six TSM day-conferences at Oundle, attended by teachers from all over the UK, and many associated TSM training days elsewhere in the UK and other countries.

Oundle School is the second largest co-educational boarding school in the UK, 30 miles west of Cambridge. The Mathematics department has been involved in using technology since the early days of the BBC micro, and has developed the use of a classroom computer connected to a TV display as a teaching tool.

Autograph is a suite of interactive programmes for teaching secondary Mathematics, created over the past 10 years by a team of teachers and pupils at Oundle School.

Autograph covers pure mathematics and statistics, and includes what is perhaps one of the most useful school-level graph plotters. It has been completely re-written for the PC platform as a dynamic co-ordinate geometry package. It is best known for being 'teacher- friendly', with intelligent default entries throughout.

MEI – *Mathematics in Education and Industry* – is a teacher-led group that provides examinations, support materials and INSET to over 600 schools and colleges in the UK. It is now the second largest provider of the modular Mathematics 'A' level examination.

Case Study 5: The State of Electronic Publishing and its Impact on the Availability of Source Materials for Higher Education and Research

Barbara Kirsop
Electronic Publishing Trust for Development,
Stanfield House, Lincolnshire, UK

Introduction

This case study reviews the present status of electronic publication and assesses its likely impact on the exchange of research information generated in both developed and developing regions of the world as well as its availability for higher education. Although the study focuses on scientific research, and uses a bioscience initiative as an example, the overall conclusions are generally applicable to other disciplines.

Professional ideas, research results and educational material are traditionally transmitted to peers throughout the world through the printed publication of journals. The rising costs of publishing on paper and the resultant cancellation of journals by libraries (Figure 4.9), which are themselves facing budget cuts, creates the need to reconsider the overall position. The situation is serious in all libraries, but is particularly acute in developing countries where librarians are trapped between the rise of commercial journal costs and the demands of their users.

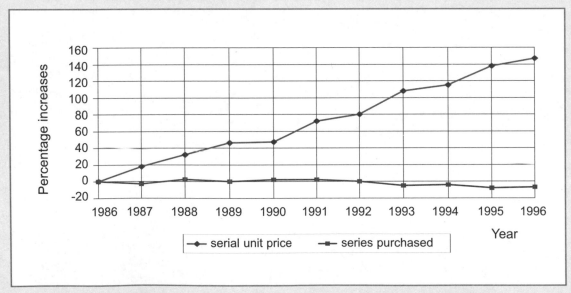

Figure 4.9 The Rise in Costs of Journals, and Its Impact on Subscriptions, 1986–96

According to the Association of Research Libraries, scholarly publishing and academic resource coalition (SPARC) libraries spent 124 per cent more in 1997 than in 1996 for 7 per cent fewer titles. The organisation is launching a programme1 to collaborate with partners in the development of 'prestigious, cost-effective alternatives' to existing journals; the programme also aims to restore publication rights back to the author.

In this climate, the advent of the internet, the world-wide web (the Web) and electronic communication is leading to a major reconsideration of the best way to exchange research material and an analysis of whether information distribution can be substantially enhanced and cost savings made by use of electronic media. Since the late 1980s a growing number of electronic publishing initiatives have been started; many information exchange mechanisms have become established and other models are under development. The technical opportunities have in turn led to a re-evaluation of what is important in scholarly publication and how the internet can contribute to the evolutionary process.

It seems clear now that electronic publishing is a positive development that is here to stay. At a recent International Council for Scientific Unions workshop,2 the general view was that in five years' time electronic publication would dominate printed publication, at least for academic journals. However, the best way to make use of the new technology is still under debate and research communities, librarians and publishers are actively considering how to change working practices to meet the new technological advances.

The opportunities are revolutionary and offer mechanisms for the academic communities in developing countries to increase hugely the visibility of scholarly research generated nationally. Many of the present difficulties met in transmitting research results by printed publications, and the feeling of academic isolation commonly experienced by researchers from national/regional institutions in developing countries, can be overcome by electronic means, leading to global distribution of research and teaching material and involvement in international academic activities.

The Internet and the World-Wide Web

The growth in use of the internet has been phenomenal, although estimates of the numbers of sites on the network vary wildly. Because of the unstructured architecture of the network, control is difficult and it is not surprising that standards are still under development. Locating material of interest becomes an increasingly important issue and concerns are raised about the identification of reliable material for academic purposes.

However disorganised general information may appear, the infrastructure and technology have been in use by the academic community for a considerable time and a good measure of organisation of academic information is already in place. Vast quantities of high-value scholarly information are already available on-line to the international community and it is now difficult to imagine a future where research and education will revert to a solely paper-based environment.

'The ability to build and mobilise knowledge capital will become as necessary to development as mobilisation of physical and financial capital in the years ahead ... We must be determined that all countries of the world participate equally and benefit fully from the global information revolution.' (John Wolfensohn, President, World Bank)

There has been criticism that the internet will increase the gap between the 'haves' and 'have-nots' because much of the necessary infrastructure is not in place in countries where the need for information is greatest. This problem was addressed by the recent Global Knowledge '97 (GK97)3 Conference in Toronto, hosted by the World Bank and the Government of Canada and sponsored by UNESCO, UNDP and others.

The first regional follow-up of the GK97 Conference was the organisation of a conference in Addis Ababa4, in June 1998, on Global Connectivity for Africa, at which governments, development agencies, banks, companies and the International Telecommunications Union discussed the need for the development of goals and projects that would make a positive impact on public telecommunications in Africa. There is no doubt that the value of ICT (Information and Communications Technology) for development is well recognised and priority is being given to measures that support it. It can be expected therefore that the infrastructure for the support of electronic publishing will develop steadily, providing a growing number of opportunities for its use. With time and training, the knowledge gap can be closed.

The internet supports the world-wide web which provides a powerful mechanism for on-line linkages to different information resources. Not only can sites providing similar kinds of information be linked, but links can be made from terms used in documents to related data held elsewhere – either on the same computer or on different computers on sites in different parts of the world. The hypertext reference standards that have been developed provide a common command for insertion into text, allowing readers to click on the link and be transferred instantaneously to the other sites of interest. The potential this offers for academic research publications and distance learning initiatives is discussed further below.

The technology for the preparation of documents for the world-wide web is readily learned. Courses are increasingly organised (References, e.g. 5) for the conversion of text and graphics for the internet, and on-line tutorials are available for self-tuition (References, e.g. 6). 'Web authoring' tools are commonly available as part of word-processing software, and web-browsing software for both searching the internet and reading web documents is accessible from the internet itself from many software sites. Once the infrastructure for ICT is available, the cost of technology for electronic publishing is not prohibitive.

The Present Status of Electronic Publishing

The potential of electronic publishing has been recognised for over a decade, and during this time commercial publishers and academic organisations have been considering the impact of the technology, both on the enhancement of information exchange and on the economic changes that follow.

Commercial Publishers

Commercial publishers have been developing mechanisms that continue to allow control of documents and that are generally precise electronic versions of the printed publication. They are using the internet as a new and powerful distribution mechanism that has the potential to greatly expand markets. The fear has been that the traditional print-based market will be damaged by electronic mechanisms, and publishers have held many meetings to discuss the dangers of copyright infringement; of losing control of the material; the quality of publications (are peer-review procedures commonly practised in print-based journals applicable?); images and technical data problems; archiving and indexing problems, and – crucially to the industry – costs and pricing policies.

Many of the major commercial publishers have now made their publications available electronically, and the University of Toronto's Centre for Instructional Development technology web site (References, 7) has an exhaustive list of these, as have other sites. The development of a parallel means of publication has required new investment and, as a consequence, the prices of electronic versions of printed journals have either increased, remained the same or been only marginally reduced. Technical issues are being resolved, and controlled formats, such as that provided by ADOBE, have been largely adopted. Some services have been established that provide electronic distribution for other, usually smaller, publishers (References, e.g. 8), providing economies for the publishers and experience in the e-pub market.

It is widely found that up-take of the electronic material is slow and a number of reasons for this are propounded. Undoubtedly the paradigm shift from a print-based to an electronic environment will take time as publishers, distributors, libraries and end-users change their working habits and learn new skills. Additionally, mechanisms for different payment structures have to be put in place and library committees in universities, institutes and companies have to be persuaded that the change is beneficial. The whole revolution is taking place within a framework of falling library budgets and more stringent accounting procedures so that it is inevitable that change will take time.

Society Publishers and Their Academic Members

In general, scholarly societies that are also publishers are more concerned with the academic advantages of electronic publishing than are commercial publishers, and are driven by their members' demands. They too are affected by the increasing costs of traditional publishing and must recover development costs, and are taking a closer look at 'alternative' publishing opportunities offered by the web. Many of the major and most innovative developments are coming from societies, and in some regions initiatives have been launched that bring together government, societies, libraries and users into a consortium to develop a national or regional service, such as the Virtuoso partnership initiative in Canada. Many of these initiatives are listed on the Toronto Web Site (References, 7).

In science, the opportunities for adding value to the traditional published page are being widely welcomed. The ability to provide links to references, images, video clips and, most excitingly, to the major international public domain databases changes the static printed document completely, into an interactive on-line information resource. Users can click on the term 'tyrosine phosphatase', for example, and be transferred from the document to the entry for this enzyme in the Swiss database (EXPASY) for a volume of related data; click on the gene 'ade1' and reach the sequence databases in the USA or Europe; click on the name of a micro-organism and link to a database with further information on its properties and how to acquire a sample of it; click on a reference to the previous lecture in a course and immediately down-load it.

Secondary datasets, not suitable for print publication because of their volume, can readily be made available through the web linking mechanism. Discussion forums, news-groups, supplier databases, e-mail, and other services can all be provided in association with a journal – or a collection of topic-related journals – forming a specialist location on the internet that is user-driven, international and interactive (References, e.g. 9). The potential for making maximum use of the web's linking capabilities is thus very great and is gradually becoming incorporated into publications as standards are being discussed and accepted.

Many society publishers are using formatting standards such as the hypertext mark-up language (HTML) (References, 6) and standardised general mark-up language (SGML) (References, 10). Information on these, and software for using the internet with Netscape and Internet Explorer Web browsers, is readily available from many internet sites, largely free of charge.

Authors from many disciplines are contributing to the debates on the merits of electronic publishing and its potential for improving information exchange. Traditionally, scientists and other academic authors publish the results of their research in printed journals, the copyright of which is held by the publishing company or the society. They are not generally paid for their contributions and the benefits arise primarily from the knowledge that their work forms part of the archived body of public-domain information and can be built upon by others for the public good. Additionally, authors anticipate accelerated career developments as a result of publications and this can be affected by the numbers of times their papers are cited by indexing, abstracting and other organisations – a policy that is currently being questioned since the number of times a paper is accessed is not necessarily the same as its scholarly worth.

However, the real wish of authors is for 'paternity' of their research and future association with it. They are less concerned with copyright issues than with international contacts, partnership prospects through increased visibility and a general wish to be part of the international academic society through their publications and ideas. Authors also want global distribution that is not limited by economic constraints. Additionally, the potential for facilitating access to secondary data, references and international databases is of fundamental importance and interest since this opens the gate to a wealth of subsidiary information often difficult to obtain. For teaching and training, the linking potential is very clear as teaching resources on the internet (books, manuals, check lists, lecture notes) are increasingly available and again lead to collaborative educational and research initiatives and course developments.

Authors are always concerned with quality and the need to conserve authenticity and accuracy and, thus, the need to preserve the peer-review system (or develop it into a more transparent system). There have been a number of meetings (References, e.g. 11) at which this issue has been discussed and it is now generally accepted that the traditional review process can only benefit from greatly speeded electronic communication between authors, publishers and referees. Moreover, new review mechanisms using a wider review community are being developed (References, 12), and these could lead to more open and improved means of assessing quality.

Libraries

While libraries welcome any developments that have the potential to reduce the costs of providing a comprehensive service to their users, it is recognised that traditional ways of providing this service must change and that there must be investment in development that can be off-set against future savings. In the developed countries there are already major programmes (usually nationally based) to establish the 'electronic library'. Such services provide multi-media facilities, on-line access and a platform of training and awareness activities to facilitate use. It is anticipated that, in time, the current investment will be rewarded by cheaper journals; better and more comprehensive collections; enhanced scholarly features (such as hyperlinks), and shelf-space savings. It is recognised that if electronic technology provides better information exchange, then this is the way to follow, at whatever pace resources currently allow.

Libraries in less developed countries face many problems at present, but can begin to visualise the benefits that electronic publishing could offer in the longer term. The technology offers the possibility to catch up and move towards more equitable access. Governments, national educational departments and teaching and research institutions need to work together to give priority to infrastructure development, perhaps working on a regional basis. Awareness and training are required to mobilise action. The author/reader communities should be involved in developments since their academic demands will be the driving force for progress. For libraries with slim resources, the eventual change from high-cost print-based journals to lower-cost electronic material is a development that must be welcomed wholeheartedly, while accepting that progress may be slow. Already steps can be taken to establish training and exchange programmes so that a body of receptive librarians is in place when the potential can be realised. Any suggestion that this new technology is not applicable for developing countries should be considered against the evidence of the great number of ICT programmes described in the GK97 Conference and already successfully under way, and the Electronic Publishing Trust for Development's activities described below.

On-Line-Only Electronic Publishing (O-L-O)

A further development that is emerging is the publication of journals that are only available electronically. This clearly has great economic impact in terms of cost-savings and a number of studies have now been carried out to assess the costs of electronic publication compared with print publication (References, 13, 14). Costs depend on the way the o-l-o publishing is carried out; the overheads that have to be met; whether archiving can be managed centrally; how much responsibility for formatting the documents is borne by the authors; the technical complexity of the documents (mathematical or scientific equations and terms), and whether a uniform style is desirable or necessary. It seems to be accepted that the major costs are in start-up and that these diminish as the software development is completed (though this is always liable to further bursts of development to keep up with new technical advancements). There are eventual cost savings to libraries by eliminating the problem of shelf space shortages, once computers and networking are in place, and further advantages in terms of single document purchase (not restricted to o-l-o journals, however), searching capabilities and monitoring usage for library policy decisions.

Several o-l-o journals have been set up and are becoming accepted by the academic community as the number of authors willing to support the new medium grows. It seems inevitable that this trend will accelerate as confidence in quality is confirmed.

A further issue under consideration is whether the existing annual subscription/document delivery charging system best serves scholarly publishing. It is being debated whether authors would be willing to pay a modest publication charge in return for which they would receive free global distribution; unlimited access to all other papers published in the same journal; retention of the copyright. Cost recovery models of this kind are already under discussion or operational.

Journal distribution on disk offers another means of reducing costs, leading in time to the elimination of printing costs altogether. The time is not right for this in many regions where (a) a printed publication is prestigious and an encouragement to scientific development (but see Developing Countries, below), and (b) an adequate computer-based infrastructure is lacking. Nevertheless, the advantages in moving away from print-based publication are attractive in terms of both economics and academic enhancement.

A Summary of Advantages and Remaining Uncertainties

The advantages and remaining uncertainties of electronic publishing are summarised in Table 4.5.

Table 4.5 The Advantages and Remaining Uncertainties of Electronic Publishing

Advantages	Remaining uncertainties
• Speed of review and speed of publication (therefore advantages in paternity, especially in highly competitive research areas)	• Economics of e-pub versus print-pub (especially for commercial publishers)
• Added-value through associated online subject-orientated services (discussion fora, secondary data, multi-media resources, suppliers' databases, e-mail, etc)	• Archiving technology (still need standards to be developed)
• Associated gateways to international public domain databases through hyperlinks	• Web organisation to ensure visibility
• Global distribution/international visibility	
• Flexibility in use for the reader (graphics/ no graphics, abstracts only, full text only, optional links, etc.)	
• International collaborative opportunities/ sharing information	
• Eventual cost savings	

The Opportunities for Developing Countries

Another aspect of electronic publishing of major importance to developing countries is the potential for greatly improving the current poor distribution of research results generated in universities and institutes. Because of the rising and increasingly prohibitive costs of printing and distributing scholarly journals, print runs are often small and international visibility is consequently poor. Authors become unwilling to commit effort to publishing in local journals since they feel that their research will remain largely invisible (References, 15).

The result of this is that essential information often remains unpublished since, except for the most prestigious institutes where research is fashionable (e.g. molecular biology and genomics), it is difficult for scientists in developing countries to have papers accepted in the mainstream journals published in the developed world. This is of particular concern in such disciplines as medicine (tropical medicine, epidemiology, emerging new infectious diseases), environmental sciences (including bioremediation, biocontrol, conservation), agriculture or taxonomy, where a global picture is required.

Electronic publishing offers an excellent opportunity to overcome the visibility problem. With only a relatively small investment in equipment (modems, scanners), software (image-handling, optical character recognition, web-browsing and formatting – some of which is available direct from the internet at no cost),

'The invisibility to which mainstream science publishing condemns most Third World research, thwarts the efforts of poor countries to strengthen their indigenous science journals – and with them the quality of research in regions that most need them.'
(Richard Horton, editor, The Lancet*)*

and training (again much of which is available on-line), local publishers can make their material web-compatible and distribute it on-line, hugely increasing visibility and greatly encouraging the academic community. The benefits, particularly to society publishers, are clear.

The British Council has adopted a major programme of support for the electronic publication of academic publications in developing countries (References, 5), and is focusing on raising awareness of benefits and initial hands-on training. It supported the participation of the Electronic Publishing Trust for Development at the GK97 and Toronto scholarly publishing conferences in 1997. The regional networks and support staff of the British Council form an invaluable resource for moving things forward and the programme is already under way.

The Electronic Publishing Trust for Development (EPT)

In recognition of the great potential of electronic publishing for the distribution of essential scientific information generated in developing countries, the EPT was established as a UK Charitable Trust at the end of 1996. Its formation was initiated by Bioline Publications (References, 9) – a not-for-profit, scientist-run system for the on-line distribution of bioscience and medical journals. Further information on the Trust, its activities and links to the journals can be found on its web site (References, 16). The distribution system used, as well as demonstration papers and additional services associated with the journals, can be viewed on the Bioline web site (References, 9).

At the time of writing (1998), the full text and graphics of 15 peer-reviewed bioscience journals from developing countries are available on-line. Some have been supported by such organisations as the Southern African Book Development Education Trust and the International Network for the Availability of Scientific Publications, others by Bioline itself. The journals currently on-line are:

· *African Crop Science*, Uganda
· *African Journal of Neurological Sciences*, Kenya
· *Biotecnologia Aplicada*, Cuba
· *Central African Journal of Medicine*, Zimbabwe
· *East African Medical Journal*, Kenya
· *Ichthyological Bulletin*, South Africa
· *Ichthyology Special Publications*, South Africa
· *Indian Journal of Experimental Biology*, India
· *Indian Journal of Biochemistry and Biophysics*, India

- *Indian Journal of Marine Sciences*, India
- *Insect Science and its Application*, Kenya
- *Memorias do Instituto Oswaldo Cruz*, Brazil
- *Transactions of the Zimbabwe Scientific Association*, Zimbabwe
- *Tropical Biodiversity*, Indonesia
- *Zimbabwe Science News*, Zimbabwe

Not only does distribution on the internet provide hugely increased visibility for these journals (the free abstracts and other material on the Bioline system are accessed by some 50,000 unique sites annually), but scientists are encouraged by greater recognition of their work and professional collaborative studies may be formed between researchers around the world. The listed journals have originally been formatted for the web by Bioline Publications, but gradually the technology is being transferred to the local publishers so that the system becomes sustainable.

The publishers of the journals benefit from the use of a well-established on-line distribution system. All material on the Bioline system is available through annual subscriptions or by single document purchase. Hypertext links are routinely incorporated, adding scientific value and providing gateways to international databases. A number of additional on-line facilities are available. The system aims at maximum flexibility in use and gradual cost reduction, and is currently also available by e-mail. It is managed by scientists and is driven by the needs of scientists.

Analysis of the usage of the journals on the Bioline system shows a steady increase in interest as users become familiar with the journal contents, and as a body of material is made available on-line. It is likely that in time additional annual subscriptions and single-document purchases will provide income to meet electronic publication costs.

The EPT is looking for other publishing partners and is working to set up resources to support new initiatives and sustain existing structures.

Future Prospects

Undoubtedly electronic publishing offers great opportunities for the more equitable, faster and academically enhanced distribution of knowledge. The benefits for publishers and the academic community in developing countries are very clear. Technology and its transfer are moving fast and, as the shift from a paper-based system to a more electronic mechanism takes place, cost savings can be foreseen. For research scientists, teachers, medical practitioners and all other academic workers, the web provides enormous opportunities to re-think the best way to distribute essential information. Many models are already operational or under way, and it is expected that within the next five years electronic publishing and distribution mechanisms will dominate.

It can be predicted that throughout the next decade academic researchers, librarians and publishers will be working together to raise awareness of the benefits of electronic publishing, developing standards, learning new technology, installing on-line systems and developing networks for the organisation of initiatives on a national, regional or international basis. The comparatively low cost of the technology and the emphasis now being placed on ICT infrastructure support are such that countries with economic difficulties will not be disenfranchised.

'Developing countries should recognise their role in the global community and give top priority to producing local information in strategic areas such as: policy and legal documents; reference and text books for primary and secondary schools; scientific documents and journals.' Canhos et al. (References, 17).

As new initiatives – often bottom-up, society-driven – emerge, organisation of academic publishing on the web will be required. The web visibility of these initiatives will best be raised by the establishment of umbrella sites for disciplinary or regional publications. In developing countries there may be benefits in the development of regional centres of expertise that can support e-pub training, act as an intermediary between publishers and host computers, and feed into umbrella sites.

It is likely that the structure will emerge gradually as initiatives evolve, the economic situation becomes clearer and the end-user community adjusts to the new environment. The EPT has considered the scheme shown in Figure 4.10 as a possible model.

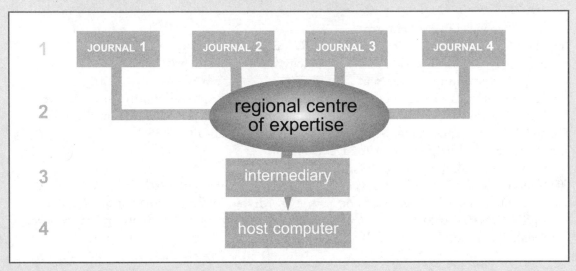

Figure 4.10 Electronic Publishing Organisation Model

References and World-Wide Web Addresses

1 'Journal prices lead libraries to back less costly initiatives', *Nature*, 25 June1998, News.

2 International Council for Scientific Unions, workshop on 'Economics, Real Costs and Benefits of Electronic Publishing in Science', April 1998 (Report in Press, programme on-line)
   http://www.lmcp.jussieu.fr/icsu

3 Global Knowledge 97 Conference, Toronto
   http://www.globalknowledge.org

4 Africa: Connectivity Conference, Addis Ababa, 1–4 June 1998
   http://www.un.org/depts/eca/globalc/index.htm or
   http://www.bellanet.org/partners/aisi/gloalc/index.htm

5 British Council
   http://www.britcoun.org/gk97/index.htm

6 Beginner's Guide to HTML:
   http://www.ncsa.uiuc.edu/General/Internet/WWW/HTMLPrimer.html

7 Comprehensive Electronic Publishing Site
   http://citd.scar.utoronto.ca/Epub/1997.html

8 CatchWord Service
   http://www.catchword.co.uk

9 Bioline Publications
   http://www.bdt.org.br/bioline

10 Introduction to the SGML Primer
   http://www.gca.org/stanpub/primer.htm

11 *Electronic Publishing in Science: Proceedings of the Joint ICSU Press/UNESCO Expert Conference*, February 1996, D. Shaw and H. Moore (eds), Paris: UNESCO and ICSU.

12 'Winners and losers in the global research village', P. Ginsparg, in ibid.

13 'Comparing electronic journals to print journals: are there savings?', Janet H. Fisher, MIT Press, Scholarly Communication and Technology Conference, April 1997.
   http://www.arl.org/scomm/scat

14 'The future of electronic journals', H.R. Varian, University of California, Scholarly Communication and Technology Conference, April 1997.
   http://www.arl.org/scomm/scat

15 'Characteristics of the publishing infrastructure of peripheral countries: a comparison of periodical publications from Latin America with periodicals from the US and UK', V. Cano, *Scientometrics*, vol. 34, no.1, 121–38, 1995.

16 Electronic Publishing Trust for Development
   http://dspace.dial.pipex.com/bioline

17 'Electronic publishing and developing countries: trends, potential and problems', V. P. Canhos, D.A.L. Canhos, S. de Souza, B. Kirsop, in *Proceedings of the Joint ICSU Press/UNESCO Expert Conference*, February 1996, D. Shaw and H. Moore (eds), Paris: UNESCO and ICSU.

Notes

1 Journals from a country/region, or journals associated with a particular discipline.

2 Regional centre with experience in electronic publishing procedures; can act as training centre and also co-ordinate transfer of journals to host computer (probably through an intermediary organisation).

3 Intermediary organisation that standardises material into the specific requirements of the host computer (bibliographic referencing, file numbering, hypertext links, graphics formats etc); transfers all files to the host computer; manages user registration; handles subscriptions; returns income to publishers; manages usage statistics; provides general promotion.

4 Host computer and software development. Note: There may be various models of the above arrangement, depending on available expertise. The elements can be in different countries (cf. Bioline arrangements: publishers in several countries, the intermediary in the UK and the host computer in Brazil, each element providing specific expertise). More than one function could be combined at a single site. Such a distributed system makes best use of skills.

5 Summary Overview and the Way Forward

Current Realities and Future Challenges

There can be little doubt that for developed and developing countries alike, education has become one of the top priorities for individuals, communities and national governments. It has also become a major area of focus for international organisations, aid agencies and non-governmental organisations. It seems that in a period of rapid change and uncertainty education has become something of a repository for our hopes for the future. There are great expectations about the contribution that education can make in such diverse areas as alleviating poverty; resolving conflict; promoting democracy and good governance; improving economic productivity and competitiveness; safeguarding cultural integrity; enhancing international understanding; and strengthening justice, peace and equality. In general terms, there is a renewed faith in the role of education in helping to create the kind of future in which the majority of people would benefit from an improved quality of life in the economic, social, political and cultural spheres.

It is difficult to fathom the diverse rationales advanced for this renewed faith in education and the expectations associated with it. Indeed, some cynics have argued that there is nothing really new about this. In the past, education has frequently been cast in this same role of repository of our hopes for a better future. Despite undeniable progress and achievements for which education can justifiably take some credit, much of what is wrong in the world today can be attributed to the failure of education to deliver on promises and fulfil expectations. Most developing countries have invested heavily in education in the past, but this has not translated into sustained educational achievements. Instead, their education systems are now in danger of being paralysed by inefficiencies and overwhelmed by a plethora of demands and expectations. The failure to provide equitable access to reasonable quality education for all is perhaps the most evident example of unfulfilled promises. It has often given rise to a sense of betrayal and inequality, which contributes to the social tensions and conflicts that have plagued many societies. It has meant that individuals have not been able to achieve their full potential; communities have remained trapped in underdevelopment, and nations have not been able to make full use of their human resource potential. Ineffective pedagogy and poor quality education have widened the gap between developed and developing countries in educational achievement and outcomes. Similarly, weak management of education systems has resulted in a catalogue of wastage and inefficiencies that have almost crippled some systems and undermined confidence in public education. In the face of such damning indictment, it might well be asked what is the basis for the renewed faith and confidence in education as the main repository of our hopes for the future?

There are at least three lines of argument that can be used to justify such renewed faith and expectations. First, education has brought about very significant achievements, even in the most under-developed societies. In every sector, in every country, there are qualified and trained nationals carrying out essential professional functions and meeting most of the nation's human resource requirements. This is clearly the result of relentless efforts at capacity-building over the years, involving education and training. Moreover, individuals, households and communities have experienced the transforming power of education in terms of improvements in earnings and general quality of life from one generation to the next (inter-generational mobility). At the international level, it can be argued that education has helped to promote better understanding and tolerance across different cultures, political ideologies and economic systems. In short, the world has seen and experienced enough of what can be achieved through education, to justify renewed faith in it. The main challenge for the future is how best to spread the self-evident benefits of education more widely, in order to fulfil the expectations of individuals, communities and nations of the world.

The second line of argument has to do with the growing ascendancy of knowledge and information as the key factors shaping and determining growth and development in the modern world. As the world moves from the old era of industrialisation to this new age of knowledge and information, education has become increasingly important as the key determinant of life-chances and development prospects for individuals and communities everywhere. To a great extent, education has always been an important engine for economic development, social mobility and cultural advancement in society. The age of knowledge and information is ushering in something of a renaissance, which is characterised by a new sense of urgency and radical change regarding the role of education as a repository of our hopes for the future. The twentieth century was characterised by an explosion in knowledge and information, and, more importantly, we continue to witness an exponential growth in the knowledge and information available to us. Given the unprecedented nature of these changes, one thing stands out in this whirlwind world of expanding and changing human knowledge. It is our ability as individuals, communities and nations, to cope with the challenge of constantly acquiring all the changing knowledge and information we need to function, collaborate and compete successfully in every sphere of life. This is not a matter of choice or expediency. It is nothing short of an imperative for survival and development in the modern world! One of the greatest challenges raised by the education renaissance, therefore, is how we should package knowledge and promote learning in a manner which adequately addresses this survival and development imperative. In short, innovations in policies and strategies that relate to the design, delivery and management of education programmes will be at the heart of the renaissance in education.

The third line of argument concerns advances in technology that are fuelling the change from an industrial age to an era of knowledge and information. In general, these advances have made it possible for us to use information and communication technologies in quite novel and revolutionary ways when dealing with knowledge and information. They have enabled us to transform the ways in which knowledge and information can be generated, packaged, transmitted, stored, retrieved, managed, accessed, processed and used. Consequently, we are now more hopeful that with sensible policies, sound strategies and careful planning, we can overcome some of the traditional obstacles that have plagued education. For instance, it may be possible to spread the benefits of education to most people, regardless of location and circumstances. It may also be possible to empower individuals, communities and nations to make more informed choices and select from a wider range of options, in deciding how best to meet their own learning needs. Such possibilities have given rise to a renewed sense of optimism about the role of education in shaping the future.

While this renewed optimism may be justified by the kind of arguments outlined above, it should also be noted that education in most countries is fraught with problems and difficulties that pose a serious challenge to its possible role in shaping the future. For all the achievements catalogued over the years, we are still in a world in which close to one billion people are illiterate and over 130 million children cannot have access to primary education. The plight of these millions is increasingly regarded as intolerable in an era of technological surfeit which makes it much easier for information and knowledge to flow rapidly and freely across boundaries. We also live in a world in which the knowledge and information gap between societies and within societies continues to widen in parallel to the existing gap in wealth and development. There are serious challenges relating to this growing equity gap, between countries and within countries, in terms of access to and benefits from education. There are also threats relating to the risk of economic and cultural domination as some societies become richer and others become poorer in the knowledge and information age.

Against this background of current realities and future challenges, this book's main concern has been with the opportunity that we have now to make real and significant changes in education. There is a fundamental sense in which education should learn from the past and envisage the future as it endeavours to serve the present needs and priorities of society in a rapidly changing world. Technology obviously has a major role to play in this education renaissance, but change should not be seen mainly in terms of technology. The starting point for change has to be educational objectives and concerns, with technology being treated as a means to achieving goals in education. This is why the main focus of this book has been on three of the most fundamental challenges faced by many education systems, namely:

· how to spread the benefits of education to all the population, regardless of location and circumstances, in a manner that adequately addresses different learning needs;
· how to promote and safeguard an appropriate level of quality in the content and process of education to cope with the dynamics of change in human knowledge; and
· how to manage a wide diversity of education provisions for greater effectiveness and efficiency as well as to promote better integration of alternative options in the system.

In addressing these fundamental challenges, the primary focus and emphasis has been on issues, principles and practices relating to education. Technology has been considered mainly in terms of the role it can play in facilitating solutions to the problems faced by countries in their efforts to deal with these educational issues. This book has avoided the usual danger of technological determinism, by portraying technology as a tool that serves human purposes in dealing with education, rather than an end in itself to which education must conform. There has a deliberate attempt to outline possible uses of a wide range of technologies, rather than being confined to computers and the latest information-communication technologies.

Making Choices and Assessing Consequences

Perhaps the first and most important advice for policy makers and professionals who make decisions in education is that they should recognise and appreciate what is positive about their existing education system. It is easy to be cynical and over critical about the problems; and the search for solutions is a perennial task. We should not lose sight of what is being achieved in education despite the difficulties and against great odds. Overzealous researchers and reformers are urged to be humble and to recognise that a functioning education system is a miracle of social creation that should not be lightly abandoned. This is very much what Skillbeck meant when he pointed out that 'what goes on, even in the poorest schools, is infinitely more complex than what a computer can do'.

Despite the problems of access, quality and management, positive achievements are a routine feature of most education systems. Every day, and in many ways, young minds are being inspired; skills are being acquired; values are being shaped; characters are being formed, and new generations are being initiated into the universal heritage of human understanding, and introduced to the rich culture of knowledge and skills that can transform lives. The challenge for decision-makers is to develop the kinds of policies and strategies that would make these sorts of positive achievements a reality for the great majority of their citizens, on a routine basis. We need to have a deep understanding of how education systems function to promote these achievements, and where they are failing to meet the expectations of various interest groups. Without this, there is a danger that we may be lured into adopting 'quick fix' solutions to the many problems which undoubtedly exist in education. The main focus should therefore be on educational issues and the kind of challenges that need to be addressed, rather than technological fashion and the desire to be in line with the latest tools.

The second piece of advice for policy makers is that they should acknowledge and accept that the shift to an era of knowledge and information is a reality that cannot be reversed or diluted. There are several dimensions to this shift that pose a challenge for education systems. For instance, the shift implies that individuals will need to be able to take much greater responsibility for accessing and selecting the kind of information and knowledge that addresses their needs. Education systems which remain very prescriptive and restrictive will become counter-productive in the face of such new demands. In much the same way, the desire for continuous learning, as a survival imperative in a rapidly changing world, means that we will have to liberalise the time-bound and place-bound nature of our current education process.

Third, decision-makers need to be acutely responsive to the fact that the new information and communication technologies have the potential to bring about a positive revolution in education. This is already happening in many societies as these technologies impact on the ways in which we package, disseminate and access the wide range of knowledge and information now available to us. There is no getting away from these developments, and every country must make choices about the use of these technologies in education. It is not a matter of whether or not to invest in such technologies, but how and when to do so, in a manner that will best address the challenges facing different education systems.

Fourth, decision-makers would be well advised to be wary of the dangers of technological determinism in attempting to deal with educational problems. There are strong pressures to introduce modern technologies in education. These are fuelled partly by a fear of being left behind in the information and knowledge revolution that is being driven by these very technologies. This fear is constantly being reinforced by the intensive hype surrounding the use of modern technologies and the apocalyptic fate awaiting societies that fail to invest in them. In this sort of climate decision-makers need to have a sense of realism as well as of urgency. Fear needs to be tempered with hope and confidence if sensible choices are to be made about investing in technology for education.

Finally, it needs to be emphasised to policy-makers that the shift to an era of knowledge and information has given rise to a renaissance in the ideology of education as the main repository of our hopes for the future. This represents a unique opportunity for addressing the fundamental problems and challenges facing different education systems. It is an opportunity that will be squandered if the wrong choices are made, and faith in education is once again undermined by unfulfilled promises and a failure to deliver on expectations. The risk of squandering this opportunity makes it imperative that the role of technology in addressing educational challenges should be considered in the broadest and most holistic context. Sound educational thinking has to take precedence over the glitz of technological gimmickry and the lure of simplistic imperatives.

Against this background of broad advice, there are specific questions that policy-makers will have to tackle as they try to make sensible choices about investing in technology for education. These have been highlighted in various ways throughout this book, and can be summarised in terms of the following examples:

- *Why is the use of technology being considered in the first place?*
  - What is the education problem that needs fixing? (E.g. increased access for certain target groups; improved pedagogy and quality; efficient management of the system, etc.)
  - How much do we know about this problem and all the factors that affect it?
  - What have we learned from past efforts to deal with this kind of problem?
  - How clear is it that the use of technology will make a difference?
  - What are the expectations of different interest groups concerning the use of technology to address this problem?
  - Do we really need to bring in technology as an important part of the solution to this problem?
  - What would happen if we did not introduce technology in this regard?
- *What are the available options, should we decide to use technology in our efforts to address this problem?*
  - What exactly is the technology expected to do in educational terms?
  - What is the range of available technologies (old and new) that could be used to achieve the desired outcome, in educational terms?
  - How wide is the gap between different technologies in terms of their total costs and requirements, as well as their effectiveness in helping to achieve the educational objectives concerned?
  - How well do the different technologies fit in with the current education culture and what people are already familiar with in the society?
- *When is the appropriate time to introduce the chosen technology in education?*
  - What kind of preparatory work needs to be done for the chosen technology to be accepted by various interest groups? (E.g. publicity campaign, conditions of service, etc.)

- What are the technical prerequisites and requirements for introducing this technology in the education system? (E.g. infrastructure, training of personnel.)
- What are the financial and budgetary implications that need to be cleared as a basis for introducing the technology?

· *How should the chosen technology be introduced into the education system?*
- Is it feasible to introduce the technology throughout the system in one go?
- Is it more realistic to take a phased approach to get it fully implemented?
- Should the technology be introduced first in pilot or trial form?
- Should it be confined to certain levels or sub-sectors of the education system?
- Is it preferable to introduce the technology in model form in a limited number of settings, so that it can be replicated as and when feasible?

· *Who should pay for the various aspects of introducing the technology?*
- What are the equity issues that need to be addressed in terms of who pays for it and who benefits from it?
- What is the role of communities in helping to meet the costs involved?
- Is there a case for involvement of the private sector?
- How do the costs involved fit in with other investment priorities in education?
- Is there likely to be any political fall-out over the use of public funds to pay for introducing the technology?
- How far can the various costs involved be afforded by those who are expected to pay for introducing the chosen technology into education?

These examples of critical questions that policy-makers need to face are simply one side of the investment issue. The other side has to do with the consequences of choices made and decisions taken about investment in technology for education. It is therefore very important that attention should be given to the possible consequences of various choices and decisions. For instance, introducing a new technology in education might require significant investment in new infrastructure, equipment, supplies, training the users, meeting maintenance and other service costs. It could also produce savings and efficiency gains – for example in terms of fewer teachers needed and better use of learning periods. In addition to such direct costs and benefits, the technology might result in new patterns of work for staff; demands for increased remuneration, and changes in the way learners and teachers interact. In general, both positive and negative consequences result from the choices we make about investing in technology for education. These need to be anticipated in an informed manner, and carefully analysed in the later stages of the decision-making process. The main concern should be with whether such choices and their consequences will make for real improvements in education, or simply result in the kind of showcase 'technological solution' which fails to penetrate and transform the education system. There are far too many examples of these kinds of innovations which are enthusiastically cited in the literature, but which often amount to little more than isolated enclaves of 'good practice' that do not take root in the system as a whole. This is yet another example of failure to meet expectations in education. At best these kinds of show-case innovations can inspire us with ideas about what is possible, but we need to ask why so many of them collapse when we try to take them to scale.

The opportunity available now for addressing the fundamental problems of education is far too valuable to be wasted on showcase innovations. This is why policy-makers and their professional advisers have to deal with issues in education and technology from first principles and in a holistic manner that takes account of education in its broadest sense, now and in the future. There are always difficult choices to make, but this is what bold and responsible leadership is all about. Policy-makers and their professional advisers must therefore resist the temptation to surrender their responsibilities to the technology lobby or the development pessimists. Quick-fix solutions and showcase innovations should never be used as a substitute for the intensive analysis, bold vision, realistic assessment and pragmatic choices that are at the heart of good decision-making.

Shaping a Vision and Cultivating a Climate

All countries, developed and developing, need to have a sense of vision to guide policies and strategies in investments in technology for educational purposes. Many countries are already envisaging a future in which most of their citizens will have unprecedented access to knowledge and information through the exploitation of advantages offered by technology. This kind of vision has become one of the most important driving forces helping to determine the national goals and objectives for education in many countries. For instance, educational goals and objectives in Namibia are being greatly influenced by the vision of a 'learning society'; in Barbados by what has been termed 'EduTecVision 2020'; in Malaysia by the vision of a so-called 'ICT super-corridor', and in the United Kingdom by the vision of a 'knowledge-based economy'. In each of these cases a vision has been espoused by the political leadership and has captured the popular imagination, as well as inspiring professionals in education and other fields. This is a very important stage in any process of major innovation or reform. Indeed, it should be regarded as critical when it comes to making investments in technology that are intended to help tackle some of the most fundamental problems in education.

The first stage in transforming vision into reality is to create a climate in which the right sorts of policies and strategies can begin to take hold and flourish. Policy is essentially to do with priorities and resources for achieving long-,term goals. There will always be many priorities in competition for scarce resources, and much depends on the right climate to ensure that a particular set of priorities is given higher weighting and allocated more resources than others. For instance the idea of investing in modern technologies can be difficult to justify as an educational priority in many developing countries where there are more fundamental problems of too many deprived schools, too many unqualified teachers and too few children at school. In such circumstances it can be difficult to talk about high-cost modern technology, unless a clear link can be made between this kind of investment and the fundamental problems evident to people in society. Yet a climate of crisis brought about by these very kinds of problems can make officials desperate for quick solutions, and cause them to turn to new technology as a panacea. This is often the origin of later disappointment with promising innovations in education.

Strategies are concerned with the most effective and efficient ways of achieving priority objectives. To be of any use, strategies must be feasible and have a realistic chance of being implemented successfully. This means that the conditions and circumstances of the situation must be carefully analysed to determine what is most appropriate. Even with the best strategy it is important to have alternatives that offer a fall-back position when things go wrong during implementation. What seems very logical and straightforward might turn out to be quite impracticable for all sorts of unforeseen reasons. Similarly, what works well in one setting (country or institution) would not necessarily work in the same way in a different setting. The key point about strategies is that there is no way of guaranteeing that they will work, apart from actually implementing them. This is why it is sometimes prudent for institutions and countries to pilot or try out different strategies on a small scale before making final decisions about major investments in technology for education.

Sharing Experiences, Expertise and Resources

One of the most pervasive consequences of globalisation is the sense of interdependence in the economic, social, cultural and political spheres of development. In this regard, breaking down the barriers to free trade results not only in investment flows and new resources, but also in the greater interaction of social norms, cultural values and political traditions from different societies. There are both positive and negative consequences associated with globalisation, so difficult choices have to be made about opening up the borders of an education system to external influence. In the positive sense it is desirable and enriching for every education system to be open to external influence, in order to learn from others and engage in mutually beneficial exchange. However, in the negative sense this kind of external influence can breed intellectual dependence as well as cultural invasion that might result in an education system being disconnected from its national context.

For instance, many of the benefits of the African Virtual University are quite clear. It can make higher education accessible to many people in Africa who cannot afford the time and cost of full-time university attendance. Learners can get the academic courses of their choice from the best professors in an American university, through the net. They can even gain qualifications backed by an American university without travelling out of their own country. However, this also raises the issue of the role of local professors in terms of job security and intellectual integrity. More importantly, if there is no reciprocal flow of knowledge from Africa to America there is even greater harm being done to the future of education in Africa. This perpetuates the syndrome of Africans as mere consumers, rather than a people with recognised expertise, capable of contributing to knowledge and intellectual development in various fields. The dilemma, therefore, is how can Africa benefit from the considerable knowledge and expertise of others in the field of higher education, without sacrificing its intellectual soul or mortgaging its academic future? Is it possible to share without being trapped into long-term dependency and jeopardising the fragile intellectual capacity that has been built up over the years? These are fundamental policy questions which show that there needs to be more to the African Virtual University concept than the use of new technologies to enable learners in Africa to access courses in American universities.

The point is not that there is anything basically wrong with sharing and learning from others. On the contrary, this is a highly desirable and potentially beneficial way forward in the process of tackling fundamental education problems. What is being argued, however, is that if benefits are to be realised and the possible negative effects are to be minimised, there needs to be careful analysis and informed decision making. Examples of the areas in which there is considerable scope for sharing expertise, experience and other resources include the following:

· *development of courseware on a collaborative basis by groups of countries to ensure optimum quality and cost effectiveness.* This was one of the recommendations by the Malaysian delegation at the 13th Conference of Commonwealth Education Ministers (13CCEM) in Botswana in 1997;
· *sharing of expertise in the technical areas of installing and maintaining equipment and systems related to various technologies.* This can be through training of personnel and various forms of technical assistance, or simply by contracting out such functions to capable private-sector providers who may also be required to train local staff;
· *training in the preparation of pedagogical materials for self-learning and distance education.* This is one of the areas in which the Commonwealth of Learning (COL) is already providing considerable service to many countries.

Developing Concrete Policies, Plans and Strategies

Ultimately each country needs to address the issues of investment in technology for education in concrete terms. This means sensible policies must be developed, feasible plans drawn up, and effective strategies designed for translating such policies and plans into reality. All of this calls for informed decision-making, and it is this that has been the main focus of this book. The concern has been with the fundamental educational problems facing most education systems, and the role that technology can play as part of the solution to these problems. The contention has been that far too many countries adopt policies and strategies driven by technological considerations rather than by educational requirements. In other words, technological determinism has been far too pervasive in our thinking on change and reform in education. This is not necessarily all negative, since it is sometimes worthwhile putting a few computers into an institution and seeing the various uses to which they are put by staff and students. And some countries have simply been concerned that staff and students should develop a familiarity with new technologies that are rapidly becoming common in the wider society, particularly in the workplace. This has usually been seen as an adequate reason for introducing computers into education institutions. Generally, however, it is now clear that institutions and countries need to shift from this kind of *ad hoc* trial and *laissez-faire* approach to new technologies to a more long-term perspective and a more systematic way of developing policies, plans and strategies. Otherwise there is a danger that education will once again be the subject of disillusionment and a scapegoat for development failures, as promises remain unfulfilled and expectations fail to be met. This is why it is critical that policy-makers and their professional advisers should be clear about the educational purpose underlying any decision to introduce technology into the education system. This has been the central theme of this book, and it provides the best platform on which a genuine dialogue and exchange can take place about investment in technology.

Case Study 6: Information Technology and Education in the Caribbean

Roderick Sanaton
Caribbean Telecommunications Union, Trinidad

Introduction

Information technology (IT) encompasses various factors. The Information Technology Professional Society of Trinidad and Tobago (ITPS) suggests that IT includes matters concerned with the furtherance of computer science and technology, and the design, development, installation and implementation of information systems and applications. The Information Technology Association of America (ITAA) defines IT as the study, design, development, support or management of computer-based information systems, particularly software applications and computer hardware. Simply stated, IT refers to the dissemination, processing and storage of information, primarily through the use of computers.

Today advanced microelectronics and computer-based information and communication technologies are at the heart of social and economic transformations in industrialised countries. The links between computing and telecommunications have been growing in the Caribbean too. Information gathering, processing, storage and transmission over efficient telecommunication networks will be key elements in enabling the Caribbean to develop into a 21st century information society. Many reforms and improvements are needed in both public- and private-sector education and training institutions to create a work-force that is trained and skilled in IT. IT can improve education and training techniques. It facilitates distance education, making possible active rather than passive learning through the synergy of sound, video, animation, graphics and texts. It can strengthen and expand upon work in the area of computer studies; develop national and regional capability for human resource development; generate and develop adequate means of providing open learning to as wide a cross section as possible of society; satisfy the universal need for intelligence; facilitate computer literacy; complement teaching, and so help to eliminate the idea of 'imperfect teaching'. However, the results of surveys on IT in education[1] show that there is a high and unsatisfied demand for IT professionals. IT skills are in extremely short supply. Dr Kwame Charles affirms that this demand is exacerbated by the international shortage of IT professionals and the threat that this poses to the local IT human resource base.

IT in education is used predominantly for meeting the requirements of the Caribbean Examination Council (CXC) syllabus and similar examinations, and for computer literacy and office productivity (word processing and spreadsheet usage) courses. Little or no emphasis is placed on the teaching of skills required for software development or computer maintenance.

In the past decade Caribbean countries have experienced difficulty in adapting new technologies. Major problems include high costs; inability to obtain access and upgrades, and the re-skilling of the labour force to manage and operate such technologies.

Primary and Secondary Education:
Programme Trends in the Private and Public Sectors

Introduction

IT is a resource which can be used to facilitate learning and teaching in all subject areas. Ideally, it should not be tackled in a small number of specifically timetabled lessons in the curriculum, but integrated right across the curriculum to ensure that all school leavers are IT literate. The drive towards IT in education should not be seen as the provision of a Computer Studies option at secondary level. This option should be tailored for those pupils who have a specific interest in the technical perspective of IT with an eye to pursuing further education or employment in the field.

IT in Primary Education

It has at last been generally recognised that computers and IT should be introduced at primary level. Yet the use of IT in Caribbean primary schools is almost non-existent. Few countries have been able to set up the infrastructure needed to train young children in the use of IT products.

Five per cent of government-run primary schools in Trinidad teach IT programmes.[2] In the few cases where IT is used, it is employed either as an administrative tool or as an aid in the various subject areas. In Trinidad there is a general problem of lack of adequate security in primary schools, so computer equipment is kept in the Principal's office under 'lock and key' and used only for administrative functions, whereas IT should be used to stimulate and encourage learning.

There has been an attempt to provide four primary schools in Tobago (Bethseda, Golden Lane, Mt Gomery and Belle Garden) with internet access. These schools are being renovated to accommodate the necessary equipment, as part of a project by the Telecommunications Services of Trinidad and Tobago (TSTT) to provide 33 schools with free internet access. However, due to the high cost, TSTT could not offer this to all the schools; others get access to the internet at a 50 per cent rebate. This development has been slow because the schools are unable to meet the 50 per cent cost requirement. They hope that corporate citizens will 'adopt' a school and provide them with a number of access hours, bearing in mind that they have to pay only half of the full cost.

In Trinidad the Government has embarked on a project to equip all primary schools with computers to ensure that everyone leaving the education system is computer literate. The Government has set up an Internet Learning Centre to provide computer training to teachers. It is hoped that eventually such a facility will be established in each community; however, problems related to existing infrastructure need to be resolved. In the few cases where computers are already in schools, Quadra Mac 605 systems are used. These machines have limited hard drives and are outdated. Teachers and students use them for computer aided programmes.

In Belize[3] just six of 245 government primary schools (2.45 per cent) teach IT programmes. The figure for private-sector education is higher: six of 32 existing primary schools (18.75 per cent). Most of the funding to provide existing infrastructure was obtained from international sources. There has been co-operation with local and foreign internet and IT service providers to give free internet access to primary and secondary schools. Yet Belize faces similar problems regarding a lack of trained IT teachers, infrastructure maintenance and resource facilities.

St Lucia[4] does not yet use IT at primary level. 25 per cent of government secondary schools and 33.3 per cent of private secondary schools have IT facilities, but IT programmes are not compulsory. Funding for IT is obtained from the Government, private donations and school fund-raising programmes. Here too outdated computers are an obstacle to learning; there is a need for proper maintenance, and for the creation of a body or institution to facilitate updating, problem-solving and the implementation of IT programmes in schools. Internet access is provided to schools with IT facilities.

Generally, IT is still severely under-utilised and there is much scope for development in the primary education system throughout the region. Stand-alone personal computers (PCs) with the provision for dial-up internet access are most commonly found in primary schools. However, it has been recognised that IT should be introduced extensively at primary level, and that it should not be limited to mere computer literacy, but should include such skills as project management, database management, data communications and networking that are needed to widen the IT base for future professionals.

Noteworthy of mention is the EDUTECH 2000 project being implemented by the Government of Barbados, designed to make all primary school students computer literate by the year 2000. If other countries in the region were to adopt such policies, similar strategies would certainly be needed for IT and human resource development.

IT in Secondary Education

As the progression of IT from primary to secondary level occurs, students begin to explore IT and manipulate applications, so usage at this level is far more widespread. IT subjects are included in CXC ordinary and advanced level examinations[5] and cover a range of issues. Students must learn

- to take a business's financial records (prepared manually) and computerise them;
- to write a computer programme using training in Basic and Pascal Programming;
- about hardware and software systems and networks.

An increasing number of schools in Trinidad and Tobago are pursuing courses in IT.[6] Student enrollment for CXC IT examinations increased from less than 100 in 1993 to almost 600 in 1998. GCE Ordinary level enrollments increased from 400 to nearly 500 over the same period. However, at GCE Advanced level, enrollments seem to have fallen since 1993. Yet analysts affirm that the increasing number of secondary school students pursuing courses in IT bodes well for the future of the industry in Trinidad and Tobago as it shows that interest in the field begins before university. There is, of course, a need to create IT appreciation much earlier than secondary school.

Many secondary schools in the region are equipped with computer labs and software to satisfy the requirements of the CXC syllabus. They have realised that such equipment is a valuable asset and have begun to offer adult literacy classes in the afternoons and at weekends. Thus maximum use is made of the computer facilities outside the traditional school hours of 8 a.m. to 3 p.m.

Some secondary schools are even contemplating establishing web pages, but this is fairly expensive and schools (e.g. Bishops Anstey, Tobago) have only been able to design the page.

In Belize, more attention has been paid to IT at secondary level than at primary level. IT programmes are taught at 75 per cent of both government and private schools, and are compulsory. Students are taught basic computer knowledge and use of applications like word processing, spreadsheets and database, together with programming in Basic or Pascal. Most schools offer RSA and CXC external examinations. Harry Noble, of Belize Information Technology Systems Ltd., affirms that IT should have a greater impact in education generally: few schools use IT as a teaching tool. He cited Mopan Technical High School as an example to emulate. This institution uses IT as a multimedia teaching tool to simulate experiments in science.

Education sectors in the region may be inspired by the example of St Kitts, where every secondary school is equipped with computers. However, there are only five secondary schools on that island. The Grenadian Government has embarked upon a programme to equip all secondary schools with computer labs.

Proposals for IT in Schools

The deployment of IT in primary and secondary schools should be governed by a dynamic strategy which entails

- *initial teacher training and in-service training*: In order to introduce IT as a cross-curriculum teaching and learning aid in both primary and secondary schools, appropriate courses should be provided for all teachers, since they will be affected by the necessary changes in curriculum and methodology. This entails the establishment of suitable courses for student teachers and teachers in service. With regard to initial teacher education, it is important that all new graduates have received adequate training in the use of IT in education. This implies that the necessary courses must be introduced into the B.Ed. and other related programmes of study. With regard to in-service training, two kinds of courses should be conducted:
  1 for teachers who lack the necessary background, but who wish to teach the Computer Studies option at secondary level. A suitable evening diploma course can be designed;
  2 for all teachers on the use of IT as a teaching and learning resource within their areas of specialisation. These courses can be conducted gradually, on a yearly basis, anticipating at each step the requirements for the following year;
- *courseware development and evaluation*: New computer-based material does not necessarily obviate the use of other kinds of material. All courseware has to be designed, developed, customised and evaluated in line with curricular content. Its purpose is to help the teacher convey the message more effectively and the student to learn more efficiently and holistically.

  There is a spectrum of development between traditional, paper-based courseware and state of the art multimedia, computer-based learning environments. More sophisticated courseware becomes available from international sources, and must be evaluated and customised to local needs. Other courseware must be developed locally, especially for subjects with a local or regional dimension;
- *curriculum development*: The gradual introduction of IT in education should be seen as a catalyst to assess and upgrade the curriculum throughout the education system. The extent to which the curriculum is revised depends on the pedagogical philosophy adopted as a matter of policy. IT can be introduced in schools simply as a tool to support 'chalk and talk', or it can be viewed as the platform for radical change in curricular activity to support group-work and fast and easy access to

knowledge in its various forms. A middle path would be gradual adaptation in the curriculum according to the training of teachers, and the education system as a whole. A directorate should be established in each country's Department of Education to carefully design and monitor the evolution of the curriculum;

· *system installation and support*: As developments in technology are occurring rapidly, the purchase of systems should be incremental and upwardly compatible. It is vital that the purchase of systems does not encounter bureaucratic bottlenecks which will force the purchase of the 'latest old technology'. In time a scheme should be adopted to allow retooling and redeployment of outdated equipment. The investment made to install the initial IT infrastructure in schools must be maintained over the years to periodically augment and upgrade the facilities;

· *research, monitoring and evaluation*: IT adoption is the first step. Ongoing research must be conducted to monitor, evaluate and direct the process. The introduction of IT in education is only justified if the benefits alluded to earlier are achieved. The University, in collaboration with local Ministries of Education, should support a team of educationalists to foster links with international institutions working in this field. Local initiatives should be kept in perspective of achievements abroad.

These activities must be integrated, and simultaneous with the refurbishment of schools and the computerisation of school administration.

Tertiary Education: The University of the West Indies (UWI)

The tertiary level of education seems to be taking the greatest strides, with IT a major component of the curriculum. At the University of the West Indies (UWI), for example, it is being used in distance education, increasing access to all UWI programmes for students who have difficulty attending a campus. IT is enabling communication among the different segments of the University, and with other institutions within and outside the region. Further, all business education courses have an IT component. It is being used as a tool in Data Analysis, Engineering, Health Services, Architecture (geographical mapping and imaging), Hospitality (as a facilitator for menu planning and clothing design), the Social sciences (for analytical purposes), and the Arts (for record keeping and word processing).

UWI recently[7] hosted a conference on educational technology, at which the Vice-Chancellor, Professor Nettleford, spoke of the UWI/CARICOM/UNDP initiative to provide IT training to faculty and students. Other speakers focused on the new paradigms for education; the possibilities and pitfalls of education technology; technology as a learning partner; the influence of technology on leadership and management; global access to library and information resources, and internet or web-based education. Several presenters from North American and British universities explained how their online courses function. They are developed on the internet, using 'web course tools' or 'course management systems', which guide the instructor to create his or her own course. Students can register for the course online; pay for it by credit card; access course material (textbooks, lecture notes, tutorials, tests, etc.) at any time and from anywhere in the world. Global teams of students work on team projects without ever meeting or knowing each other. Evaluation and student tracking can be done online so that the instructor is always aware of how the students in his or her 'virtual' class are doing. The internet is creating a new kind of tertiary institution – 'Laptop University' commented Dr Kwame Charles.[8] Entrance requirements include the possession of a computer – preferably a laptop or notebook – internet access and competence in the major application software in general use. Information and communications technology (ICT) will revolutionise education (from primary to tertiary level) as it is revolutionising work, business and life in general.

UWI Institute of Business (IOB)

At the Institute of Business (IOB) the concept of ICT is applied, yet full use is not made of the technology. Much of the documentation is sent via mail. Facilitators are sent to the respective countries for approximately two weeks for discussions with students. Upon the facilitator's return, communication continues by means of the internet.

UWI distance learning

In 1997 UWI's Distance Education Centre (UWIDEC) introduced its Distance Learning Programme to meet the learning requirements of the people of the Caribbean. Students may pursue several university programmes at a distance and are not required to attend the physical site of the campus.

In order to widen access to their programmes, UWI has made use of a variety of educational methodologies: self-study printed materials supported by audio and video cassettes where applicable; face-to-face tutorial sessions, and interactive audio teleconferences. Computer assisted learning packages, e-mail, and access to the world-wide web are currently being developed by UWIDEC.

The programme serves 17 Commonwealth countries in the Caribbean and covers Anguilla, Antigua and Barbuda, The Bahamas, Belize, British Virgin Islands, Cayman Islands, Dominica, Grenada, Jamaica, Montserrat, St Kitts and Nevis, St Lucia, St Martin, St Vincent and the Grenadines, Trinidad and Tobago, and Turks and Caicos.

Perhaps one of the most common reasons given in favour of this form of instruction is that it is an excellent opportunity for bridging the gap between urban and rural education. Throughout the region, many of the facilities are located in urban areas, and major sections of the population are deprived of the opportunity to pursue an education at either primary, secondary or tertiary level. Greater use of distance learning methodologies would allow the region to educate more of its citizens and narrow the gap between urban and rural education. The result would be the creation of a *total quality region* and the attainment of sustainable development.

In view of the rapid increase in the amount and cost of traditional academic instruction, the increasing globalisation of the economy and culture, and the growing role of information-age tools, distance education is becoming a viable option for pursuing academic qualification. However, due to the constraints on accessibility and affordability, designers of course material within and outside developing countries will have to pay attention to hybrid delivery methods and developing alliances in developing nations.

Technology and programme content

The use of IT at UWI and at other tertiary institutions in the region is not restricted to the computer literacy function. It enhances graphical preparation and presentation of course materials, and is being incorporated into the curriculum of several disciplines, especially in languages, social sciences and human resource development training. In

Engineering, IT is used as a training tool: some experiments are difficult and dangerous and computers are used to simulate an experiment before the students carry it out .

Professor Charles Cadogan of the Department of Computer Science, Mathematics and Physics at UWI's Cave Hill Campus foresees changes in the Department's present course content. He noted that the first group of students in this area will graduate in July 2000. The B.Sc. IS/IT will be reviewed and the Certificate in IT will be upgraded in anticipation of more advanced students. In addition, an M.Sc. IT is to be introduced.

Use of Infrastructure

Professor Cadogan cites insufficient support staff and difficulty in the procurement of site licences as the main problems encountered by the Department in the use of computer-aided learning (CAL) packages. Similar problems are encountered on the other UWI campuses. At Mona, Jamaica, Professor Han Reichgelt also identified the shortage of staff as a major obstacle. Similar views were expressed by Sharon Kinch, Executive Assistant at the Centre for Management Development (Eastern Caribbean) Inc., UWI. She stated that in general it is difficult to find a good IT lecturer.

Other Initiatives in IT Education

It has been suggested that while there is significant evidence of the use of IT in the education sector, its use varies at the different levels. At primary and secondary levels, the emphasis is on introducing and exposing students to various uses of IT. Training at secondary level allows for the immediate transfer of skills from school to the workplace, and creates an awareness of the extent of the impact of IT on our everyday lives.

Use also differs between the public and private sectors. The private education system recognises a need to be innovative and to remain on the 'cutting edge'. It has a strong research base and can determine demand. The public sector generally cannot keep up with the market in the same way, and has difficulty staying up to date. The private sector's success may be due to facility availability, or it may be more enterprising. Whatever the reason, the private sector is able to adapt more readily to changes.

At the University of Technology (UTECH) in Jamaica, IT usage is extensive. All the business education courses have an IT component. There are also several computer and IT educational initiatives, including the Institute of Management Sciences (IMS), the Institute of Management and Production (IMP), and the Jamaica Computer Society (its objectives include getting computers into schools).

The Royal Bank's Institute of Technology (ROYTEC)

Some educational organisations in the region are totally IT dependent. For example, at the Royal Bank's Institute of Technology (ROYTEC) students are taught Secretarial Services and are exposed to word processing and spreadsheet preparation. Emphasis is placed on use of the internet. In particular, ROYTEC offers a Bachelor's Degree in affiliation with the University of New Brunswick. This degree is heavily dependent on the internet as the primary means of transmitting data for the course. IT is also being incorporated into the institution's marketing department which uses the technology for advertising and consultancy. The school also has an associate degree programme in Management Information Systems which involves substantial IT knowledge.

Other Distance Learning initiatives

Distance education is generally taken to mean independent study, or open learning based on self-instruction materials. The key element is the separation in space and time of the the teaching and learning activities. Distance learners are supported at-a-distance by trainers, tutors or subject specialists and, informally, by other learners taking the same course. Traditionally, distance education referred to correspondence study; the delivery tool was the mail. IT has broadened distance learning to include audio, video and computer technologies.

Tele-education refers to a variety of applications of telecommunication technologies and services for educational purposes, including anything from televised educational programming to individual researchers using remote databases, and covering all levels from elementary to adult education. There is often a video component, which generally starts with one-way video and two-way audio.

Online education is a step forward in the realm of tele-education systems. With the emergence of computer-based communication systems such as the internet, online education has enhanced the distance education experience. Tutor support can be almost instantaneous; interaction with one and/or all other students is readily obtainable; distance and cost for the transmission of messages has become irrelevant, and the educational material can be interactive, multimedia, and available online. The rapid migration of distance learning courses to the internet is manifest evidence of this transformation.

Internet-based courses have a number of advantages over those delivered via satellite. First, the cost of setting up the system is dramatically different. Satellite transmissions require earth stations relatively close to the point of delivery to reduce the cost of ground telecommunications connection. They are generally one way. Internet transmission can be achieved for a fraction of the cost of satellite, and is always interactive.

Second, the reach of the broadcast of each system – and therefore the economies of scale that can be achieved – is also quite different. A satellite transmission reaches only the geographical area covered by the footprint, whereas an internet broadcast has no geographical limitations once basic communication infrastructure is in place.

The benefits that apply for tertiary education are applicable to postgraduate training and continuing education. Internet distance education programmes in developing countries are not only conceptually viable, but practically feasible. Building the required communication infrastructure is generally the easiest, and in the long run the cheapest part of the process. What seems to be much more difficult to achieve, in terms of time and cost, is the sustained production and supply of content. In other words, the successful introduction of new technologies such as the internet into education depends largely on the quality of course materials and their relevance in the local context. In developing countries most of the educational content available is not suited to distance/online education. Most of the distance/online educational content available is from developed nations, which often makes it unsuitable and inappropriate to developing countries' needs.

The current thin educational content available over the internet does not mean that demand is also thin. With the rise of new electronic media the patterns of information consumption in some developing nations are changing, and the appeal for internet news and general information is growing at a fast pace *vis-à-vis* that delivered by traditional media. But if the demand for news over the internet is experiencing a rapid surge, then the rise in the demand for educational information and content is unprecedented.

Awareness of Distance Learning in the Caribbean

Throughout the region there is little awareness of the distance learning programme, except at the tertiary level. Perhaps this is because most courses offered through distance learning are for first and higher degrees. In countries where interviews were conducted, there was no mention of the principle being used as a means of post-primary training.

The programme is fast becoming an option in many countries because demand exceeds supply of further education facilities. The distance learning programme is being used to bridge the gap between those who are able to obtain a tertiary education and those who are not.

The Benefits and Costs of the Distance Learning Programme

A distance learning system has many benefits for our region. Yet this form of instruction is expensive because there it is difficult to develop the appropriate infrastructure, capacity and institutional responses to change. Another perceived problem is the lack of intimacy and absence of physical interaction.

Use of Distance Learning

Instances of use of distance learning are:

- *St Lucia:* The Sir Arthur Lewis College is planning for the use of distance education via video conferencing.
- *Jamaica:* UTECH has been taking steps to implement this programme. The pilot project is expected to be in the area of business administration, and it is anticipated that this will eventually branch off into the other academic disciplines. UWI offers assistance in designing products.
  Few other institutions offer distance education using IT. Bob Sempel of UWI notes that at present Jamaica is more of a recipient than a provider of the distance learning initiative. He affirms that there is a need for more of this kind of education, since all the major educational institutions are located in the capital. Distance education would help to bridge the gap between urban and rural education.
- *Trinidad and Tobago:* ROYTEC's programme in Management Information Systems and Business Administration is offered in collaboration with the University of New Brunswick. The Ministry of Information, Communication, Training and Distance Learning recently began its distance learning programme which will promote the use of this non-traditional form of educational instruction.
- *Belize:* Distance learning is not widely known in Belize. It is used sporadically by the Teacher's College. Harry Noble, of Belize Information Technology Systems Ltd., affirms that Belize has a real need for distance learning programmes, especially in tertiary education.

Multi-Purpose Community Centres: Suriname – A Case in Point

The Telecommunication Corporation Suriname (TELESUR) in collaboration with the ITU started the implementation of an Integrated Rural Telecommunications Project, in order to extend the telecommunication network to the interior of the country through modern technology. The pilot project was completed in May 1996.

The telecentres are installed in an area where approximately 20,000 people (about 40 per cent of the population of the interior) live in scattered villages near the Upper Suriname river. Each telecentre is equipped with two telephones, one fax machine, one computer with internet facility and printer. The most used service is telephony. The telecentres are operated by local people – two for each telecentre, who were trained by TELESUR. To guarantee a good service and to cover the costs of exploitation, including maintenance of equipment, there are plans to put the telecentres on lease.

Suriname intends to install 15 telecentres at strategic places in the interior; their locations will be determined in consultation with the Ministry of Regional Development and the medical institutions working in the interior. Video and audio broadcasting possibilities will be available in these centres for tele-education and tele-medicine purposes.

The Integrated Rural Telecommunications Project (IRTP) of Suriname is based on Programme No. 9 of the ITU Buenos Aires Action Plan (BAAP) 'Integrated Rural Development'. This programme includes the collaboration of ITU and developing countries in the long-term planning of integrated rural development at regional and national levels, rural networks and the promotion of the community telecentre concept and services. These concepts are to be implemented through the partnership arrangements involving developing countries, ITU, donor agencies, other UN agencies, regional and national organisations and other parties in the telecommunications industry.

Suriname's approach could be adopted by other Caribbean countries.

Collaboration, Co-operation and Financial Assistance

Some corporate entities are providing assistance, but more needs to be done. This section highlights some of the firms assisting in the funding of IT projects, and so promoting the use and development of IT. In some countries the Government has had to be the sole provider.

- *Belize:* There has been an initiative by the Organisation of American States (OAS) and the local telephone company to provide internet access to all the high schools. Provision has been sporadic and there is a need for a more specific plan from the IT bodies in Belize. Belize Telecommunications Ltd. has donated, and continues to donate, computers to schools on a periodic basis. It provides free internet access to primary and secondary schools and has made a commitment to provide equipment to the secondary schools.
- *St Kitts and Grenada:* The Ministry of Education is responsible for providing the schools with computers. In St Kitts all the secondary schools have computers, and in Grenada the Ministry has recently embarked on a computerisation project.
- *St Lucia:* The OAS and the local telephone company are working on a project to assist with LAN (Local Area Network) provision.
- *Trinidad and Tobago:* In Trinidad the Telecommunications Services of Trinidad and Tobago (TSTT) provides some internet service. Companies such as AMOCO and the Royal Bank have been donating computers to secondary schools. TSTT has provided a free line for internet access, and in Tobago is providing 33 schools with access (some at a 50 per cent rebate).
- *Montserrat:* Cable and Wireless donated computers to the only secondary school on the island.

- *Jamaica*: UTECH is Government-funded, and solicits grants from other sources, among them private-sector companies to which UTECH provides trained staff.
- *Suriname*: The IRTP launched by TELESUR in collaboration with ITU was financed by the Government of the Netherlands (20 per cent) and TELESUR (80 per cent).

The Role of the Private Sector

Views differ on the role of the private sector in telecommunications development. But of all the countries where interviews were conducted[9] only one felt that there was not a role for the private sector in telecommunications and IT.

The main view is that the private sector should exist for the purpose of providing services to the public. Another major role identified for the private sector is to aid in research and modification techniques. The telecommunications industry in the Caribbean is at a lower level than in developed countries. Much of the technology is standardised when it is imported and no provision is made for adjusting it to suit the needs of receiving countries. Frequently Caribbean countries pay for more than is really needed. Because the private sector is an enterprising and investing sector, it is believed it is best suited to this research activity.

The private sector is extremely forward thinking, and its involvement is, in most cases, with the end user. The private sector is therefore the best entity to advise on developmental and educational development issues. It is knowledgeable about problems being experienced, aware of the impact of new technologies, and aware of suggestions regarding the changes in the technologies in use.

Financing Electronic Education

The virtues of accessing the internet to support education are undeniable. The question is, how does a country finance it? In the USDA, for example, a programme to connect every American school to the internet by the year 2000 has been estimated at more than US$ 30 billion, plus at least US$ 5 billion annual operating expenses. The task, which is expensive for even the richest countries, can turn into a staggering burden for developing countries.[10]

For developing countries the need to migrate to electronic-based education has come at a difficult time. In most nations the state – traditionally the main financer of the educational system – is facing financial constraints and retreating from its former direct participation in the national economy. Although it is now well accepted among economists and government officials that health and education are two areas in which the state should remain deeply involved, most developing nations are finding it hard to sustain their presence in the sector and are cutting their education budgets across the board.

As nation states scale back their financing, two other kinds of institutions – multilateral lending agencies and private-sector companies – are increasing their role in the sector. In Latin America, for example, the Interamerican Development Bank (IDB) and the World Bank (WB) have committed US$ 8.32 billion in soft loans to support improvements in education in the period 1998-2000, to upgrade information and communication infrastructures and services.

The participation of private-sector capital in education is shaping up in a number of different ways. One is the increasing presence of private entrepreneurs directly involved in the provision of education at all levels, which has expanded the volume of capital available for IT in the educational system. Some of these private institutions not only have the necessary finance, but are extremely successful in raising funds. Their experience may be useful for Caribbean development plans.[11]

Other kinds of private sector involvement in education are less direct, yet no less effective or significant. A number of communication and information technology companies are looking with interest at the potential offered by the education market, and are supporting rapid growth in the use of communication and information services, such as those provided over the internet.

Education

Providers of education and training in Trinidad and Tobago[12] see the need to follow closely the requirements of industry when planning future programmes. Trends suggest that the focus will be on internet training and project management and programming courses. These courses are not necessarily driven be local market needs, but by the international affiliations of many of the institutions.

Research

Research and development are important. The needs of the market must be examined extensively to ascertain the requirements of the country and the region. Research should also seek to identify the demand for IT services. In the region the demand for IT professionals is higher than the supply. Most IT educational facilities are in urban areas; private-sector research must highlight rural demand for IT and offer positive solutions.

IT Education at Ministerial Level

Dr Kwame Charles, and nearly every other participant in the CTU study,[13] identified the need for a national enabling mechanism in each country to promote IT as a national priority. Its responsibilities should include:

- the development of national and regional IT strategy;
- the development of an IT culture;
- a national human resource development plan based on an information and knowledge-driven education system.

Encouraging investment in the IT education sector would play an important part in IT promotion. Funds could be acquired and used to access the much needed infrastructure as well as for research and development.

The study also pointed to the need for the IT industry to work closely with the various teaching institutions, especially universities and tertiary institutions to help them to supply the quality and quantity of graduates needed to sustain the industry.

Institutions should be encouraged to become more flexible in their teaching. Their rigid structures must be broken down so that they can more readily adapt to changes as they occur in the sector. Areas such as operating systems, software development and internet must be examined carefully, and the associated tools must be developed. There must be an IT human resource development programme to deal with the quality and quantity objectives pertaining to the supply of IT professionals.

Researchers note that in Trinidad and Tobago, the Ministry of Education is yet to adopt an IT education policy, although a proposal to introduce computers into public education has been in existence since 1995.[14] Though computers have been installed in many primary and secondary schools in the country, there is no systematic strategy for computer education in the national education system.

In St Lucia some government and private secondary schools do teach computer studies, but there is no body or group co-ordinating or planning the IT programmes for schools.[15] Belize benefits from the Curriculum Development Unit of the Ministry of Education. This body develops the school curriculum and buys suitable computer programmes to assist in its delivery. However, there is a problem in Belize regarding the lack of capable teachers who, as soon as they become competent, are absorbed by the private sector. The Association of School Principals seems to be the only organisation attempting to remedy this problem.

The Barbados Government has recently embarked on its 'EDUTECH 2000' plan which, as described above, is intended to make all primary school students computer literate by the year 2000.

Governments, and more particularly Ministries of Education, are faced with the difficult decision of which technologies to chose for different levels of education, distance learning included. Some pertinent questions to bear in mind are:

- *Access:* How accessible is a particular technology for learners? How flexible is it for a particular target group?
- *Costs:* What is the cost structure of each technology? What is the unit cost per learner?
- *Teaching and learning:* What kinds of learning are needed? What instructional approaches will best meet these needs? What are the best technologies for supporting this teaching and learning?
- *Interaction and user-friendliness:* What kind of interaction does this technology enable? How easy is it to use?
- *Organisational issues:* What are the organisational requirements, and the barriers to be removed, before this technology can be used successfully? What changes in organisation need to be made?
- *Novelty:* How new is this technology?
- *Speed:* How quickly can courses be mounted with this technology? How quickly can materials be changed?

The new and emerging IT trends should also be borne in mind when planning future education strategies. As noted earlier these trends include:

- internet technologies;
- network computing;
- electronic commerce;
- enterprise applications;
- digital libraries;
- knowledge management;
- component-based software development;
- multimedia;

· network security; and
· 'disintermediation'.

IT Education and Training: Social Equity

It seems obvious that there is a deep gulf between the traditional educational system, whose basis was designed in the nineteenth century, and the demands of the 21st century society, with its paradigm of production, whose development is increasingly based on knowledge, technical progress, innovation and creativity.

Governments agree that in order to increase their competitiveness, one of the biggest challenges ahead is that of transforming the quality of education: they will need more and more people with good training, and must outgrow the mechanical accumulation of knowledge.

Governments also see the need to create closer links between the educational system, the world of communications, and the sphere of work, if they are to be successful in developing internationally competitive persons. Further, the educational function of the future cannot be carried out through a routine, hierarchical structure. Autonomy, administrative responsibility, experimentation and close links with the community are needed. While decentralisation is to be fostered, the risk of inequalities which could lead to a growing differentiation between minorities trained to manage the future and majorities linked with the past, or excluded from the dynamic progress of modernity, should be avoided. Thus, together with decentralisation, emphasis should be placed on the importance of integration, social compensation for the underprivileged, and policies aimed at checking the segmentary tendencies of the market and education.

IT and Education: Trinidad and Tobago

IT education and training in Trinidad and Tobago is still in its early stages, yet many see this as a growing business. Institutions are cropping up literally overnight to try to capitalise on the increased demand for 'computer courses'. However, most of the offerings are at the lower end of the IT skills spectrum. Analysts argue that if Trinidad and Tobago is to compete in the software development market, it will have to increase its competencies in education and training in this area. The introduction into the economy of international and local software development houses can enhance the country's ability to educate and train itself.

Barbados is pursuing such a strategy by insisting that its offshore software development companies contribute in tangible ways to the development of local IT human resources, through working with UWI and professional IT bodies. Its experiences may be useful to Trinidad and Tobago's strategic planning.

Dr Kwame Charles's analysis of the IT human resource development issue makes it clear that training is inadequate. It was difficult to obtain data on enrolment and graduation for the region. Table 5.1 (page 162) shows figures from Trinidad and Tobago, and gives an idea of throughput by award and by area. The data reveals that approximately 1,122 people enrolled in the degree, diploma and certificate programmes offered by the 21 institutions studied by Charles et al. At the same time, 558 graduates emerged from these institutions with undergraduate diplomas and higher awards. 7,599 students were enrolled in a wide range of IT-related areas. Of this figure, 5,389 successfully completed programmes in these areas. These figures should not be taken as absolutes because students may have pursued other courses during the academic year.

Consider also Table 5.2. This table indicates that by far the greatest IT/computer usage is for computer literacy which records an enrolment figure of 2,225. This sounds quite good and indicates that the country has recognised the importance of IT, yet there is no mention of enrolment or graduates being produced in the field of software maintenance and development.

Input from Trinidad and Tobago also reveals that the highest academic qualification for IT professionals is at the Bachelor degree level, accounting for 41 per cent of IT staff in the country. An equally large number of people (41 per cent) have only a secondary school education, and only 11 per cent hold a postgraduate degree. Undergraduate diplomas and doctorates are qualifications possessed by IT professionals in Trinidad and Tobago, but these figures are both under 5 per cent.

An important area in IT education is on-the-job training. Faced with a shortage of IT professionals, there is a greater need to focus on human resource training. Again,

Table 5.1 Throughput of Computer Programmes by Award in Trinidad and Tobago, 1998

	Award	Enrolment					Graduates				
		1997	1996	1995	1994	1993	1997	1996	1995	1994	1993
	Associate Degree	233	105	78	91	29	61	49	7	1	0
	B.Sc	291	211	151	20	16	110	18	17	5	5
CAN	Certified Novell Administrator	25	50	75	75	50	15	38	45	49	28
	Certificate of Completion	140	132	83	83	108	119	115	83	83	108
CLP	Certified Lotus Notes Professional	–	4	4	–	–	–	2	2	–	–
CLS	Certified Lotus Notes Specialist	20	12	12	–	–	10	6	2	–	–
CNE	Certified Novell Engineer	2	5	10	10	2	2	5	10	10	2
	Diploma	15	40	40	–	–	15	40	40	–	–
	Graduate Diploma	57	25	–	–	–	25	25	–	–	–
MCNE	Master Certified Novell Engineer	–	–	3	–	–	–	–	3	–	–
MCP	Microsoft Certified Professional	200	75	36	–	–	120	45	36	–	–
MCSD	Microsoft Certified Solution Developer	15	2	–	–	–	11	2	–	–	–
MSE	Microsoft Certified Systems Engineer	30	15	12	–	–	15	5	12	–	–
	Masters	67	25	–	–	–	55	15	–	–	–

Note: Blank fields are due to unavailability of data.

Table 5.2 Computer Courses Offered in Trinidad and Tobago, 1998

Course name	Enrolment					Graduates				
	1997	1996	1995	1994	1993	1997	1996	1995	1994	1993
Computer Literacy	2225	1703	1527	1350	1191	1310	1108	942	765	616
Office Productivity	1865	1123	241	93	86	1667	1118	231	93	86
Internet User and Authority Tools	37	22	–	–	–	37	22	–	–	–
Network Operating Systems	200	50	–	–	–	65	50	20	–	–
Computer Applications	180	0	–	–	–	178	–	–	–	–
Programming Languages	40	40	40	–	–	40	40	40	–	–
PC Repair and Maintenance	45	0	–	–	–	23	–	–	–	–
Data Communications	95	80	80	–	–	83	60	70	–	–
Information Systems	315	262	133	163	108	242	235	128	153	108
Project Management	170	130	45	–	–	125	85	–	–	–
Database Management	919	402	86	–	–	927	405	86	–	–
Computer Aided Design	319	107	104	–	–	134	107	104	–	–
Geographic Information Systems (Certificate)	15	15	–	–	–	–	–	–	–	–
Desktop Publishing	79	–	–	–	–	–	–	–	–	–

Note: Blank fields are due to unavailability of data.

training to be computer literate does not suffice; emphasis should be placed on software maintenance and development. The latter is the main area of deficiency in the IT industry, as Table 5.3 shows.

Conclusion

Caribbean economies will be greatly affected by the level and quality of IT use in each country. Aptitude and skills in the application of IT tools are becoming a matter of basic literacy. As IT is set to become an integral part of life, it is important that social, technical, political, moral, organisational and economic issues and principles associated with its use are discussed adequately and practised in context from a young age. Thus IT necessitates its growing presence at all levels of education and human resource development.

Table 5.3 IT Skill Deficiencies in Trinidad and Tobago, 1998[16]

Deficiency	%
Software development skills	18
Working experience	17
Project management	17
Lack of a mix of skills	15
People/communication skills	14
Database management	11
Networking	9
Business skills	6
Web and internet	6
Other	28

Most Caribbean countries are taking steps to make IT an integral part of the education system. Difficulties should be faced and resolved with the help of a clear national education plan. Private and government sectors must strive to foster IT awareness and literacy form a young age; view IT as a cross-curricular theme throughout formal education, convey the use of IT as a vehicle for life-long learning; and create an IT-proficient work-force, and use IT to encourage an ethos of life-long education and training.

Notes

1 Charles, Kwame, et al., *An Analysis of Information Technology Human Resources in Trinidad and Tobago*, April 1998.

2 Yearwood, C., Director of School Supervision, Ministry of Education, April 1999.

3 Information provided by David Eck, Director, Curriculum Development Unit, Ministry of Education, Belize, January 1999.

4 Information provided by Mrs Esther Joseph, Statistician, CAMDU, St Lucia, March 1999.

5 Examinations in IT include CXC 'O' level Information Technology (General and Technical); Cambridge GCE 'O' level Computer Studies; Cambridge GCE 'A' level in Computing.

6 Charles, Kwame, et al., *An Analysis of Information Technology Human Resources in Trinidad and Tobago*, April 1998.

7 April 1999.

8 'Technology Transforming Education', *Trinidad Express*, 12 April, 1999, page 12.

9 CTU Working Papers: *The Role of the Caribbean Private Sector in Telecommunications Development*, September 1998.

10 In India, for example, even assuming that financing were available (which it is not), if more than 1,000 villages a year were to be connected and provided with the required hardware, it would still take 640 years to achieve nationwide coverage. See the proposal for the creation of a public communication utility at village level: Woods, Bernard, *Communications Technology and the Development of People*, London 1993.

11 *Tapping the financial market: The case of the Education Investment Corporation (Educor) of South Africa*

Educor is the largest private education institution in Southern Africa. The group, which has investments in education and personnel placement, has seen a boom in growth in recent years. The education arm employs more than 4,000 faculties to teach 300,000 students registered in its 160 branches.

Aside from traditional sources of funding (such as student fees) the company has explored new areas with considerable success. In June 1996 company shares were floated on the Johannesburg stock exchange. The promising prospects of distance education, paired with good management and excellent systems, has lead to an impressive 51 per cent rise in earnings per share in little more than 18 months.

The rise in share values reflects the impressive financial performance of the company. Educor's turnover more than tripled from December 1996 to the end of 1997, while operating profits rose by 78 per cent in the same period. Management attributes the impressive performance of the group largely to the sustained growth in the education businesses. The market capitalisation of Educor already exceeds US$ 433 million.

Reflecting the expanding business and cash availability, Educor has recently acquired the Charter Group spearheaded by the Academy of Learning franchises and the International Colleges Group (ICG). The ICG, integrated by Inter and the Rapid Results College, is a leading distance learning group with operations in South Africa, Zimbabwe and other countries in the region. The Charter Group is one of the top training institutions in South Africa and with new businesses opening up in places like Eke, New Zealand.

These acquisitions have not only doubled Educor's operations, but have boosted the group's presence in distance education over the internet. Intec in particular brings to the group state of the art internet technology and solid experience in delivery of education over the internet. Furthermore, based on the current size of the operation, Educor managers are seeking to achieve significant economies of scale in areas such as course development and advertising. The next step for the group is to go global in their operations and provide distance learning services around the world.

Source: <http://www.btimes.co.za/98/0308/comp/comp11.htm> and <http://www.woza.co.za/intec.htm>

12 Charles, Kwame, et al., *An Analysis of Information Technology Human Resources in Trinidad and Tobago*, April 1998.

13 Ibid.

14 Ibid.

15 Information provided by Mrs Esther Joseph, Statistician, CAMDU, St Lucia, March 1999.

16 Charles, Kwame, et al., *An Analysis of Information Technology Human Resources in Trinidad and Tobago*, April 1998.

The Contributors

Dr Cream Wright

Cream Wright is Special Adviser and Head of the Education Department at the Commonwealth Secretariat in London, UK. His current areas of expertise include educational planning, action research, curriculum development, project design, education evaluation, teacher education and technical and vocational education. Cream Wright has extensive insight and experience in the field of education and development, having worked in over 20 developing countries on various project assignments for many leading international and bi-lateral agencies, before joining the Commonwealth Secretariat.

Douglas Butler

Douglas Butler is the Director of the Centre for ICT Training and Research at Oundle School, UK. He has been Head of Mathematics and of Careers Education at Oundle School, but now combines teaching with running the new ICT Training Centre. He is the principle author of *Autograph* and organiser of the TSM and TTM initiatives. He has worked with teachers in many countries, notably South Africa and Singapore, on the creative use of ICT in Mathematics teaching.

Dr Magdallen N. Juma

Magdallen Juma is the Director of the African Virtual University (AVU), Kenyatta University, Nairobi, Kenya. She has wide experience in university teaching and administration, both at Nairobi and Kenyatta Universities. She has acted as a consultant in education for many international organisations, including the Ford Foundation, UNESCO and the Commonwealth Secretariat, and did pioneering work in setting up the AVU in Sub-Saharan Africa. In this regard she has undertaken consultative work for the World Bank in Zimbabwe, Tanzania, Ethiopia, Namibia and Ghana. She has published widely on education and technology, and on virtual distance learning.

Barbara Kirsop

Barbara Kirsop is a Director of Bioline Publications and Secretary of the Electronic Publishing Trust for Development (EPT), UK, which supports the electronic distribution of scientific information generated in developing countries. Barbara Kirsop began her career as a microbiologist; was President of the World Federation for Culture Collections, and Executive Director of the Microbial Strain Data Network. Her interest in electronic publishing grew from her concern at the difficulties experienced by scientists in the developing world in gaining access to scientific literature and in making widely known research from their own countries.

Roderick Sanatan

A national of Trinidad and Tobago, Roderick Sanatan is Secretary General of the Caribbean Telecommunications Union, the intergovernmental regional organisation for developing telecom policy. During the last ten years he has worked on issues of telecom policy applications for development, and has carried out research on technology transfer. He has undertaken telecom and development studies in Latin America and the Caribbean.

Dr Christina Soh

Christina Soh works at the Information Management Research Centre, Nanyang Business School, Nanyang Technological University, Singapore.

Professor Roy Williams

Roy Williams is Executive Director of Education for Development, an NGO development consultancy in the UK, and Visiting Professor at the University of Reading. From 1994 to 1997 he was the Director of SACHED Trust, a South African NGO which managed programmes in distance education, adult education and educational media. He chaired the strategic management team in the North West Province to merge six Apartheid Education Departments into one, and in 1996 chaired the South African Minister of Education's investigation to establish policy for Technology Enhanced Learning. Roy Williams held the Chair in the Department of Communication at the University of the North West, and was involved at national policy level in telecommunications, adult education and broadcasting in South Africa.